How to Read Texts

Also available from Continuum

Essential Guide to English Studies
Peter Childs

How to Read Texts

A Student Guide to Critical Approaches and Skills

Neil McCaw

continuum

Continuum
The Tower Building   80 Maiden Lane, Suite 704
11 York Road   New York
London SE1 7NX   NY 10038
www.continuumbooks.com

Neil McCaw has asserted his right under the Copyright, Designs and Patents Act, 1988,
to be identified as Author of this work.

British Library Cataloguing-in-Publication Data
A catalogue record for this book is available from the British Library.

ISBN: 978-0-8264-9287-6 (hardback)
      978-0-8264-9288-3 (paperback)

Library of Congress Cataloging-in-Publication Data
A catalog record for this book is available from the Library of Congress.

Typeset by Fakenham Photosetting Ltd, Fakenham, Norfolk
Printed and bound in Great Britain by Cromwell Press Ltd, Trowbridge, Wiltshire

For Tracey McCaw

Acknowledgements

Thanks to the many students I have taught over the last ten years or so whose lively and enquiring minds have challenged me to think in new ways.

Gratitude also to my colleagues in the English Department at the University of Winchester, whose brains I have picked and rifled thoroughly and without any shame whatsoever.

Love, as always, to Chucky and Alfredo, my favourite readers.

Contents

Introduction: Why read about how to read?

> ## Chapter summary
>
> This introductory chapter defines the scope and focus of *How to Read Texts*. It will include discussion of the differences between the study of texts at undergraduate level and earlier levels of academic work, introducing ideas about the practice and assumptions of reading, and meanings of 'the text'.

There are many books presently on the market that offer advice and tips on ways of reading 'literature'; all of these books are intended, in one way or another, to help undergraduate students through the maze of approaches and skills they need to master on their way to becoming sophisticated, informed, and confident readers. So why the need for another one? What is different about *this* book in relation to these others?

Well, for one thing, *How to Read Texts* attempts to focus more fundamentally upon *you*, the reader; it is more explicitly about *your* development. So, there is an exercise at the beginning of each chapter that encourages you to think about your own views on the particular issues to be discussed; then, there are moments for reflection throughout each chapter, when you are encouraged to stop reading and think through your own points of view on key topics (these moments are marked with asterisks in the text); finally, each chapter concludes with summative exercises to test your own learning and progress. The effect of these various exercises and moments of reflection is that throughout each chapter your own thoughts and ideas take their place within the context of the perspectives of the readers and critics of the past (from Plato through to Derrida and beyond), helping you to understand how each assumption you make about reading can be viewed in relation to the critical approaches of others.

To help you in this process, the whole of Chapter 1 of *How to Read Texts* is devoted to helping you identify and examine your own initial critical assumptions, as a start-off point for your own development across the book as a whole. This then feeds into Chapter 2, which looks at the ways in which your own creativity can have a part to play in your development as a more sophisticated and imaginative reader. The chapter encourages you to see your own personal creativity and creative thinking as at the heart of your critical-reading, and shows you how reading can be an exciting, exploratory process.

How to Read Texts thus works on developing your own self-consciousness as a reader, encouraging you to examine different 'types' of approaches to reading, and using creative-critical exploration as a means to help you arrive at more advanced, and more imaginative interpretations of texts. The aim is that you don't simply passively receive information about different ways of reading texts, but instead you participate in and engage with these approaches, and you do so self-consciously; throughout the process of your development it is important that you are aware of the implications of the decisions you make as a reader/critic.

So, *How to Read Texts* is a book written in an attempt not just to capture the methods and approaches one can take in reading texts, but also to embody the thrill and excitement of the exploratory reading process, of the quarry for meaning and understanding in prose, poetry and drama. It seeks to enliven the process of reading for those who find it more difficult, challenging, or even bemusing at times, and to illustrate that there is really no need to be intimidated by certain texts, because at its heart critically reading texts is an inclusive, rather than an exclusive activity. And once you realize this, and get accustomed to the multiplicity of ways in which the reading of texts can happen, you need never be intimidated by a text again.

What is a 'text'?

Some of you reading this book will feel that you already know what a 'text' is. As a result, it might seem as if there is little need to waste time defining it. But there are good reasons why it is worth spending just a little time clarifying what we mean when we talk of 'the text'. For, in truth, it is a term that has been keenly debated, in particular over the last half-century or so, and there are competing viewpoints as to what it means that have to be acknowledged. The intention here is to try and define a notion of 'the text' that is transparent, comprehensible and applicable, as the basis for the discussion to follow in the various chapters of *How to Read Texts*. This is not to deny other points of view, merely to recognize that when we go on to talk about 'texts' in more detail it is useful if we have a shared sense of what it is that is being referred to.

Some books that attempt to introduce degree-level reading skills and critical approaches will talk about 'literature' and 'literary works' rather than 'texts'. This is neither accidental nor incidental. In making the discrimination between 'literature' and 'writing', or between 'literary works' and 'texts', each book is making key assumptions about reading and writing, and *culture* more generally. The term 'literature', for example, has a long and contentious history. Over time there have been many different definitions of the term, ranging from 'scripture' to 'fine letters' to 'anything written'. As a result, for some, 'literature' has become 'a vague, all-inclusive term for poetry, novels, drama, short stories, prose: anything written, in fact, with an apparently artistic purpose'. In addition, it has become increasingly clear that the use of the term 'literature' is not just about referring to a particular, fixed subject matter. It is also a fundamental value judgement: '"Literature" also is an evaluative word: to say that a novel is "not literature" is to imply that it is badly written, or has for some other reason failed to achieve the status of art.'[1]

As fiction, poetry and drama came to be studied academically, and in particular with the development of the subject of English in schools and universities, teachers and critics used the term 'literature' as a way of defining which texts were to be studied. 'Literature' was what was deemed *acceptable* to teach and study, in contrast to other examples of writing that were not taught and studied. Therein 'literature' as a term embodied a measurement of artistic value, as well as at times a reflection on the moral, or even political content of the texts being judged. Increasingly, the decision as to which texts were most valued and studied became rooted in the question as to whether or not particular texts upheld favoured morals and ideas, the implication being that 'literature' should have a positive, and not a negative, impact on society. This is apparent in a critical study such as F. R. Leavis's *The Great Tradition* (1948), in which his aesthetic judgement as to the best novelists of the nineteenth century blurred into moral and political judgements as to the moral seriousness of writers and their work.

As the subject of English developed in the second half of the twentieth century in the UK, there was a reaction against the idea that 'literature' was *all* that should be read and studied. In particular, the development of Cultural Studies from the 1950s was based on the idea that rather than studying just the *classics*, the so-called greats of literary history, it was equally worthwhile (if not more so) to study a range of cultural materials. This was not just about including popular fiction (as opposed to literary fiction), but also pop lyrics, films, TV programmes, and other subject matter, such as advertising. One of the key terms that came to be used by those critics and cultural historians who were working on these 'alternative' materials was 'the text': films, TV, advertising, writing, were all seen as types of *cultural text*. And where 'literature' had tended to mean an elite narrowness in the range of work studied, 'text' didn't focus simply on the 'greats' but looked at all kinds of writing and cultural output. As a result, 'text' came to be seen as a more inclusive, more wide-ranging alternative to the traditional term 'literature'. Increasingly (to quote Roland Barthes), 'the Text does not stop at (good) Literature'.[2]

Which is why, for the purposes of this book, the term 'the text' is used rather than other comparable terms that could be used to refer to different forms of written work, such as 'literature' or 'literary writing', or 'literary works'. For, although *How to Read Texts* is concerned only with particular examples of 'texts' (novels, poems, plays, and non-fictional prose), and not film, TV, or advertising (for example), there is still an attempt to work with texts outside, as well as inside, the so-called 'canon' of English literature.

What is 'reading'?

You may be wondering how you can benefit from a book that attempts to show you how to do something you have been doing all by yourself for many years. But this book is not about telling you how to do something you already know how to do. It is about *enhancing* your reading, enabling you to read in new ways: exciting ways, intriguing ways, sophisticated and indeed at times *difficult* ways. The idea is to work beyond what I call 'reflex' reading, the level of interpretation where you almost don't realize you are doing it, and instead to help make you a more rigorous and self-conscious reader. *How to Read Texts* is about you becoming someone who interprets and critiques what they are reading thoroughly, rather than being a passive consumer of language and ideas, flicking from one page to another without absorbing the text before you.

Pre-degree reading

As you move through the different levels of education your reading evolves towards higher levels of appreciation and understanding. So that (eventually) you are able to consider characterization, setting, development of plot, and the use and effect of dialogue. At some point you will more than likely be asked to answer exam questions on some of these topics, questions that test your skills of recognition, of reading observation, of general understanding. They will involve giving a description of something, such as a character or landscape, or a contextualization of a passage in relation to the text it belongs to. These are what I call the 'what?' questions. If you are skilled at reading for the detail of texts and their language you are very likely to have great success at this level of study.

The questions might look something like this:[3]

An Evil Cradling, Brian Keenan
Read the extract printed below.
Examine the presentation of Brian Keenan's strength of character here and elsewhere in the book.
In your answer you should consider:
• choices of form, style, vocabulary and narrative viewpoint
• the ways in which attitudes and values are conveyed to the reader

Enduring Love, Ian McEwan
Read the extract printed below.

How is the relationship between Joe and Clarissa presented here and elsewhere in the novel?

In your answer you should consider:

- choices of form, style, vocabulary and narrative viewpoint
- the ways in which attitudes and values are conveyed to the reader

A Handful of Dust, Evelyn Waugh

Read the extract printed below.

Examine the presentation of John Beaver here and elsewhere in the novel.

In your answer you should consider:

- choices of form, style, vocabulary and narrative viewpoint
- the ways in which attitudes and values are conveyed to the reader

Reading as an undergraduate

When students begin undergraduate courses they almost instantly notice the difference between the sort of questions they have been asked previously (of the kind listed above) and the more in-depth questions that are posed at university level. For many students this can be destabilizing, when the range of skills that have served them well so far seem slightly redundant, or at the very least insufficient. What they don't realize is that this is a completely natural part of their critical development and that almost everyone experiences this same sense of disorientation to a certain extent.

It is important that students grasp as soon as possible the basis of the transition to degree level. For the questions are no longer of the 'what?' variety, but rather questions that invite a more sophisticated discussion of the themes and issues at the heart of particular texts; not just 'what?' questions, but 'how?' and (most particularly) 'why?' questions. So the sort of questions that were listed above metamorphosize:

'Examine the presentation of Brian Keenan's strength of character here and elsewhere in the book.'

could then become:

'To what extent can Brian Keenan's *An Evil Cradling* be seen as a novel of spirituality and/or religion?'

and

'How is the relationship between Joe and Clarissa presented here and elsewhere in the novel? [*Enduring Love*]'

could then become:

> 'The central tension in *Enduring Love*, embodied in the characters of Joe and
> Clarissa, is between conflicting interpretations of scientific progress.' Discuss
>
> and:
>
> 'Examine the presentation of John Beaver here and elsewhere in the novel
> [*A Handful of Dust*]'
>
> could become:
>
> 'Discuss the character of John Beaver in *A Handful of Dust* in terms of emerging
> class tensions in England in the 1930s.'

In each of these three cases, the focus of the question develops from a concern with what the text is doing (describing in a certain way, using language in a specific way, creating particular characters, following certain plotlines, etc.), towards a more sophisticated understanding of *how* and *why* this is being done. The questions consider the broader significances of character, event and language, implying relationships between texts' broader issues (cultural, social, political, etc.). The new questions are more demanding than the 'what?' questions, requiring different intellectual and critical skills. That does not mean that the 'what?' questions need no longer be asked, that they are redundant, but it does mean that these sort of questions should only be viewed as one stage of the reading process, rather than as the reading process in its entirety. As undergraduate students you should still be asking questions that involve such an interrogation of how a text functions, but these should no longer be the *only* questions that are asked.

So, *How to Read Texts* is about equipping you with the critical tools necessary for the transition to degree-level work, with specific chapters on the key debates, including creative criticism, close reading, biography and authorship, history and contexts, and the impact of critical theory. Along the way specific use is made of a range of critical sources, the kind of sources that it is important all undergraduate readers learn to work with. Coming to terms with these primary materials means establishing meaning for yourself, rather than becoming wholly reliant on second-hand summaries of critical ideas and debates. At undergraduate level and beyond there is an increasing need for you to ask your own questions of critical materials, and to come up with your own answers. This is why you will find a number of notes for each chapter at the end of this book; the notes are intended to direct you back towards critical source materials. The annotated lists of *suggested further reading* at the end of each chapter also give you some hints as to where your wider process of excavation and knowledge-gathering might focus.

Thus, the idea is that *How to Read Texts* becomes a springboard for your own explorations. It does not seek to be a rigid prescription, more a guide to the territory within which (and indeed beyond which) your own exciting excavations of texts can take place. The intention is that it will help you come to terms with the basics, offer you opportunities to try your hand at engaging with key issues and methods of textual reading, and give you the skills and confidence to then progress onto more advanced work. Hence the *stepping things up* sections at the conclusion of each chapter, which are intended to provide you with an early opportunity to stretch your critical legs, to use your newly acquired critical skills to experiment on and play with (in a creative-critical sense) a given text, namely Arthur Conan Doyle's 'The Man with the Twisted Lip' (which is supplied as Appendix C).

Reading and creativity

Although it is important that you learn to understand the critical writing of others, it is also important you understand that reading can be an art. Yes, an *art*. Just as with other forms of creative/critical expression, the interpretation of writing (a.k.a. reading) is a skill that requires practice and patience and imagination if you are to master it. As Chapter 2 will discuss in greater detail, to be able to offer a fresh, incisive perspective on a piece of writing can release many, if not all, of the same creative energies that would be released if you were (say) writing a poem, moulding a piece of clay, or figuring out a particular chord pattern on a guitar. The myth of the two halves of the brain, one critical and one creative, has done much to undermine such an idea, but it is now increasingly recognized by critics and thinkers that creativity has a vital part to play in all aspects of our lives.

The problem has been, to date, that universities have been slow to understand and acknowledge that the process of developing as a reader has a crucial creative dimension. Which is all the more strange because it has been fairly common-place for there to be creative writing exercises within pre-degree-level English syllabuses for many years now. Note the following, for example:[4]

---

1. Your task is to write an extract from a novel in which you aim to convey a *sense of place* and *atmosphere*.

2. Write a commentary that explains the choices that you made when writing your extract, by commenting on the following:
   - your vocabulary and style in relation to the audience and purpose for your writing
   - the content and structure of your text.

This examination paper, targeted primarily at students from 16 to 18 years of age, explicitly links the creative and the critical aspects of the study of texts and writing, pushing students towards writing creative pieces within the context of the critical examination of specific course texts and also their own work.

Yet, once these same students begin their undergraduate careers in English, the opportunity to use creative practice (i.e. writing) within a wider diet of studies and assessments narrows or else is non-existent within most universities. A fairly stark division between literary study and creative expression is maintained, meaning that most of the time if you want to write *creatively* then you study for a creative writing degree, whereas if you want to write *critically* then you study for an English degree. Many, if not most university courses in English still (things are changing, but slowly) uphold a very traditional binary opposition between what is creative and what is critical. Which means that unless your particular university allows you to divide your studies between different subjects, you're going to miss out one way or the other.

The power of reading

As soon as you accept that the process of reading is inherently creative, it becomes clear how enormously significant the reader is in the production and interpretation of texts. This explains why we should take the process of reading (and our role within it) so seriously, and also (perhaps paradoxically) why we should be so excited about it. It's not that we can no longer flick absent-mindedly through the pages of the latest blockbuster while we lie on the beach trying to cultivate a suntan. This sort of reading is absolutely permitted. Always. But it *does* mean that when we come to look at a text in detail, whether it is set reading on a particular course, or just because we feel we really want to get to grips with it, we should recognize that the process we are engaged in is extraordinary. Readers have the power to *create* meaning; not just interpret meaning, but to *create* it. To view things anew, to shed fresh light on old material, to notice intricate, previously unnoticed connections between images and ideas; these are all within the remit of our job as reader. There is almost infinite potential in the process of critical and creative reading, and we need to celebrate that. And, just as there was excitement and joy when, all those years ago, we were first able to decipher letters into words and read on our own for the first time, the development of these new critical reading skills should be thrilling and empowering.

So, *How to Read Texts* is about uncovering, developing and fine-tuning your reading through the development of a range of critical-creative approaches and skills. It is not about telling you that you've got it all wrong so far, more about showing you (through both critical and creative practice) how what you've been doing so far is only part of the story. For some students, maybe even the majority, beginning to read in a more sophisticated, more interrogative way, will be troubling at first. Troubling not just because it is difficult, but also because (for some) it requires a significantly more rigorous engagement with texts. Some first-year undergraduate students say that learning to read in this new way for a university course takes some of the enjoyment out of reading, that they can no longer just pick up a book, read through and put it down without thinking about it more deeply. 'I can't just read for fun anymore', might be the refrain. But by the end of their degree programmes these same students often remark on how they read with self-conscious rigour almost as second nature, and get much more out of texts than they ever thought was possible.

Which is a way of saying that any initial resistance you may have to this new way of reading is perfectly natural. You are being asked to interrogate material rather than simply absorb it, and that is a much more demanding mental process. However, the skills of critical and creative appreciation and understanding that you will hone and fine-tune as part of your undergraduate development will lead you towards reading texts in truly exciting ways, seeing sophistications and nuances invisible to you before, and as a consequence becoming a highly proficient, sensitive and *creative* reader of texts of all kinds.

1

Beginning from where you are – finding your critical voice

Chapter summary

This chapter will encourage you to ask a series of questions about your own preconceptions and presumptions about texts, reading, and the process of criticism. It offers a questionnaire which is designed to make you think about your own positions on a series of issues related to the reading of texts. It will then tease out some of the implications of these and how they relate to particular literary-critical approaches.

Reading objectively?

A very powerful and (it would seem) persuasive idea has characterized much of the history of literary criticism. It is still fervently held by some, although perhaps in decreasing numbers. The idea is this: that it is possible to read a text (novel, poem, play, short story, etc.) *objectively*. That there is a way of reading, of interpretation, that is not sullied by the imperfections of individual or group prejudice, of political or ideological bias, or of genetic or cultural conditioning; neither is it inescapably complicated by the slipperiness of language. The role of the reader, so the story goes, is to identify the *truth* of the text. Such a view has been implied, in different ways, by a host of critics from Plato right through to the twentieth century.

Of all the many problems we might have with this idea of the *objective* text, the most significant (because it is potentially the most damaging) is that the notion that there is a 'true' reading stifles the power of reading and interpretation. In terms of the development of reading skills, of the skills of textual appreciation and criticism, this idea threatens to hold students back from fully engaging with the complexities and delights of reading texts in new and exciting ways. All the time they are chasing the tail of the *correct* reading of a text, they are intimidated away from reading it freely for themselves.

How to Read Texts is based on the premise that it is highly problematic to talk of the correct reading of *any* text. Textual criticism is viewed as most imaginative and insightful when it is not a matter of trying to uncover the solitary truth that lies beneath the conjunction of language and form, but when it is instead about the discovery, or uncovering, of numerous different strands of meaning and interpretation: some contradictory, some complementary, but all of them (hopefully) interesting and insightful. Reading is seen not as a matter of perspective, but of perspective*s*. Not a matter of *wrong* readings versus *right* readings, more a case of *unsupported* or *unconvincing* readings versus *supported* or *persuasive* ones. Which doesn't mean that it isn't ever possible to get it wrong; but it does mean that it is never, ever, possible to get it entirely right.

The inevitability of bias

Few of us like to consider ourselves biased. But sometimes we just have to concede that we are. And in the reading, criticism and interpretation of texts, we have to accept our own bias and (at times) our *ideology*. Now, *ideology* is one of those words that is much debated and argued over. It has at times been seen as an entirely negative term, and at others something approaching meaningless. But, cutting through the complexities and political history of the term, *ideology* is broadly interpreted as meaning something approximate to a coherent *philosophy*, or *perspective*, or *bias*. Much (if not all) of what we do as human beings can be seen, in this sense, as *ideological*; symptomatic of an overarching set of values and attitudes. Reading can be seen as just such an ideological activity. It is (literally) impossible for us to read *outside ourselves*. Our point-of-view, our baggage (to coin a modern term), is with us always. When we read we do so as ourselves, from within our lives, cultures, bodily forms, etc. And if we accept that each person (reader) is different from the next, then it follows that the reading process, the process of interpretation and criticism, must by definition be slightly different for each person too.

How to Read Texts recognizes reading as biased, as based on subjective knowledge, preconceptions and ideas, as well as the reader's emotional make-up, family history, cultural background, ethnicity, gender, sexuality, class, etc. Each of us, as individuals, combines a different set of factors that input into the way we read and interpret. And none of these combinations will be identical to another. Which *should* make the undergraduate seminar room a truly wonderful place to be – all those different minds, lives, moods, *ideologies*, interacting, as each person strives for a yet more sophisticated reading, informed all the while by their own bias or perspective.

Limitations on reading

And yet the undergraduate seminar room is sometimes not like that at all, for a variety of reasons:

- Some students are constrained by the notion that somehow there is a 'right' answer.
- Some students are convinced that everyone else knows this 'right' answer and they don't; so they don't want to say anything that might make them look stupid.
- Historically, there has been a suppression of creativity within university English degrees, which has had the effect of discouraging students to be courageous and expansive in their critical thinking.

Crucially, as soon as you accept that reading is about *multiple* interpretations of texts, about lots of versions of right answers rather than a single definitive one, many of these barriers and obstructions are overcome. There is less of a need for students to feel constrained and restricted in striving for a single truth, a prescribed interpretation, an authoritative wisdom, and more freedom to explore texts on their own terms.

Using biases and preconceptions

But it is more than simply a case of accepting the fact that there are a lot of us and we each have different (but valid) perspectives. It is up to us, as evolving readers, to challenge our biases and preconceptions, to interrogate them thoroughly and on a continual basis. This does not mean that what you believe or think when you start your undergraduate course is necessarily wrong, that you have based your reading up to this point on fallacies; neither does it mean that *whatever* you think is ok, because the world is complex and each of you is an individual. What it does mean is that you need to take stock, right at the beginning of your degree courses, of exactly what it is you do think and believe, and to ask serious and detailed questions of these beliefs and ideas. It is only then that you can make a serious assessment of their validity. This self-assessment should be an ongoing part of your development as a creative-critical reader, something you return to from time to time in the process of updating or re-evaluating your critical skills.

If you do not examine your own reading practices at the outset then there are a number of risks. One is that you will become an intellectual magpie – every time you discover a new critical viewpoint or theory, you will absorb it and adopt it as your own. So when you study Freud you will become a psychoanalytic critic, a couple of weeks later you might be seduced by New Criticism, a few weeks after that by Aristotle or Longinus. Without a coherent sense of *your own* point-of-view you have no anchor to stabilize you as you get continually battered by the waves of different critical viewpoints. In addition, and perhaps more importantly, if your development as a reader and critic is not self-conscious then you have no real sense of what you believe and why. Which could leave you offering contradictory or incoherent interpretations; you could end up with a sort of higgledy-piggledy, half-articulated, makes-no-sense-at-all critical practice that works against the possibility of you offering coherent and convincing critical readings that you can truly believe in.

Thus, it is important for every student to begin 'where they are', to open up their degree-level studies by asking some detailed questions about how they have read and criticized so far, and in so doing to lay the foundation for the critical development that is to come. This is the beginning, the first step in what is hopefully an ongoing and continual re-shaping of the creative-critical self.

The undergraduate questionnaire

The questionnaire that follows is a diagnostic tool that helps you to begin to think seriously (and self-consciously) about how you read and interpret texts. The whole point of the exercise is to offer a general interpretation of your assumptions and presumptions which can then be used as the basis for your development as a reader and critic across the remaining chapters of this book. The first stage of the questionnaire asks some general questions about your reading practice. The second is more specific, and will attempt to 'place' your critical perspectives in relation to some of the key literary-critical debates relevant to the reading of texts.

Stage 1

Consider, for a few minutes each, your responses to the following:

(1) I am happy reading all types of writing, from different periods and across different genres: AGREE/DISAGREE

(2) I enjoy reading, as long as it is for fun and I don't have to think too hard while I'm doing it: AGREE/DISAGREE

(3) Reading is good for the soul: AGREE/DISAGREE

(4) Sometimes I feel insecure about what I read and think that I don't read (a) enough, and (b) the right stuff: AGREE/DISAGREE

(5) Sometimes I feel insecure about whether or not I understand the meaning of a text: AGREE/DISAGREE

Now, to the implications of your answers:

(1)   If you agreed that you do like reading across all periods and genres, excellent. The next stage for you is to ask yourself which periods and genres you feel more comfortable with, and why. If you disagreed with the statement, then (again) you need to ask yourself what it is about certain periods and genres that faze or alienate you, and try to work past your resistance.

(2)   If you agreed that reading is enjoyable only when you're doing it for fun, then ok. Any textbook that encouraged you to see reading as something other than fun would be very peculiar. But at the same time reading can also be challenging and thought-provoking, and as we move forwards as readers we need to understand the different ways in which a reader can engage with texts, and the different levels of appreciation.

(3)   If you agreed with the statement that reading is 'good' for you, then you join a long line of critics, philosophers and teachers who have said something very similar at some point over the past couple of thousand years or so of critical history. *And there is nothing wrong with such a view.* It only becomes a problem when certain texts are prescribed as a means of self-improvement and not others, as if there are texts that can teach you things and others that are worthless in this sense. And the problem is that when this happens particular types of behaviour or lifestyle are being advocated, and others rejected, and we move outside the boundaries of textual criticism into something else.

(4)   If you feel insecure about your reading and knowledge then you need to confront this feeling if you are to develop fully as a reader. Understand that when people suggest you read certain texts instead of others, there is nothing to say that they are necessarily right. You should certainly never feel that what you are reading is not suitable, appropriate, significant, or serious enough (unless, of course, you aren't reading anything at all!).

(5)   The idea that there is an objective, single and 'true' meaning of a text is closer to myth than it is to truth. It just is.

Stage 2

The next stage of the questionnaire moves you on to some more specific questions, and is intended to provide an outline of your own individual critical preferences and assumptions. It is designed to identify where you stand at the present time, perhaps at an early stage of your university studies. The aim is that this snapshot will offer a point of contrast as your own views and assumptions evolve and develop. Such self-consciousness is, as has already been said, important in an effective critic.

Beginning from where you are – finding your critical voice

Give each statement some serious thought before answering:

(1) You do not need to know anything about the historical background of a text to understand what it means: AGREE/DISAGREE/DON'T KNOW

(2) University English literature courses should include the study of texts from all over the world, possibly even those originally written in languages other than English: AGREE/DISAGREE/DON'T KNOW

(3) The meaning of the text comes through the words on the page: AGREE/DISAGREE/DON'T KNOW

(4) Some texts have a universal meaning that is relevant to all societies, both past and present: AGREE/DISAGREE/DON'T KNOW

(5) When reading a text it is important to have some familiarity with other texts in the same genre and by the same author: AGREE/DISAGREE/DON'T KNOW

(6) 'English literature' is a term that should refer to work by 'great' writers such as Shakespeare: AGREE/DISAGREE/DON'T KNOW

(7) When interpreting a text it is impossible to ignore issues such as ethnicity and gender: AGREE/DISAGREE/DON'T KNOW

(8) Genre fiction (such as romance and crime fiction) is not as well written as the classics: AGREE/DISAGREE/DON'T KNOW

(9) The critical reading of a text should focus mostly on the patterns of language and symbolism: AGREE/DISAGREE/DON'T KNOW

(10) Reading and interpreting literary texts is a critical, not a creative, activity: AGREE/DISAGREE/DON'T KNOW.

Interpreting your answers

What kind of reader are you ?

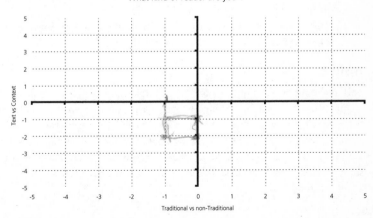

Text vs Context

Traditional vs non-Traditional

(1)   You do not need to know anything about the historical background of a
      text to understand what it means: AGREE/DISAGREE/DON'T KNOW.
      Beginning at the centre point of the graph (known as 0,0), **move one
      space to the left if you agree with this statement, one space to the
      right if you disagree, remaining in the same position on the line
      graph if you don't know.**

AGREE

If you agreed with this statement, then perhaps for you everything you need
to know about a text is contained within it. Maybe for you the words have
inherent meanings and you see it as the job of the reader and critic to decode
these. It often (though not inevitably) follows, with this line of interpretation,
that the text is seen as universal, offering fixed meanings for all time. Such a
critical position discounts the wisdom of placing a text in its historical context,
of understanding the biography of the author, or of identifying varying critical
receptions of the text across different historical periods. These things are viewed
as less important to an understanding of textual meaning.

DISAGREE

If you disagreed with this statement, it could be for a number of reasons. Maybe
you are interested in viewing texts within their historical contexts, maybe you
are interested in the lives of the authors, or perhaps you think that different
readers bring different perspectives, and it is not possible to view a text in
isolation. Whatever your reason for disagreeing, the sense that the text is not an
immoveable, unchangeable thing is being hinted at, as well as an implication that
historical-context detail has a relevance in textual reading.

(2)   University English literature courses should include the study of texts
      from all over the world, possibly even those originally written in
      languages other than English: AGREE/DISAGREE/DON'T KNOW. **If
      you agree, move one space up, if you disagree, one square down; if
      you don't know, remain in the same position on the line graph.**

AGREE

This might indicate a willingness to read past differences in national and ethnic
identities and to celebrate writing/literature as a means by which boundaries
between cultures can be overcome. On the other hand, there is for some readers
a real danger with this point-of-view, in that it can be seen as risking emptying
the idea of 'English literature' of any meaning it may have left. For, if we can
study anything, from any place and time, where do the boundaries of 'English'
begin and end?

DISAGREE

If you disagreed because you genuinely believe that texts from some cultures or national backgrounds are more worthy or relevant than others, then you might like to challenge yourself and try to establish what lies behind this assumption. Do you think this is because you just haven't read much writing from cultures other than your own? Or because you believe that English culture is of particular interest and that studying texts from beyond it is not as important? Or do you think that 'literature' is, almost by definition, in English?

(3)   The meaning of the text comes through the words on the page: AGREE/ DISAGREE/DON'T KNOW. **If you agree move one square left, if you disagree move right one square, if you don't know, remain in the same position on the line graph.**

AGREE

Many, if not most, students at pre-degree level will almost take the answer to this question for granted. 'Where else could we find meaning if not in the words?' might be the response. And this is entirely understandable. Because before degree-level the idea that language (often straightforwardly) conveys meaning goes largely unchallenged. It's one of the things that marks out the transition to undergraduate study, where the notion of language as stable and transparent suddenly becomes contested. What you must try and do is keep your mind open to the possibility that the view you held coming into your university course is not the *only* one.

DISAGREE

The fact that you resisted the idea that language controls meaning is interesting. Maybe you have already opened yourself to the possibility that there might be other points-of-view. It does not matter whether you have gone as far as thinking about the relationship between language and meaning and the role of the reader in this relationship. Just to accept that the process by which meaning is conveyed is complex is certainly enough for now.

(4)   Some texts have a universal meaning that is relevant to all societies, both past and present: AGREE/DISAGREE/DON'T KNOW. **If you agree move down one square, if you disagree move up one square, if you don't know remain in the same position on the line graph.**

AGREE

If you believe that texts have universal meanings, meanings for all time, then you are probably in the majority of readers. It is not uncommon to hear people saying things like 'this book has something really important to say to all of us'.

What you should be aware of, however, is that to accept such a universal quality in any text is in itself a political judgement. Because the problem with universalism is that it implies both that human nature is constant (you may have no problem accepting such a view), but also that morality and moral judgements are constant, and therefore people are governed by a set of rules that have been inherited from the past and which cannot and should not change. For some this is a troubling notion, one that presents a range of challenges.

DISAGREE

If you judge that texts mean different things at different times, to different people, and can be interpreted many and variously, then your view accords with that of a range of critics whose work became influential during the last decades of the twentieth century, known as critical theorists. However, to note the power and persuasiveness of this view is not to say that it is necessarily the correct view.

(5)   When reading a text it is important to have some familiarity with other texts in the same genre and by the same author: AGREE/DISAGREE/ DON'T KNOW. **If you agree move right one square, if you disagree move left one square, if you don't know, remain in the same position on the line graph.**

AGREE

To agree with this statement is to acknowledge that for you it is not enough to view a text in isolation. You may not necessarily feel that it is vital to focus upon the historical or political context of what you are reading, but you do feel that context of a sort is important. But there are obviously implications in (for example) author-centred criticism. If authorship is deemed to be significant then we are tacitly recognizing the context (and power) of authorship as a deciding factor in our critical interpretation. There is nothing inherently wrong in doing so, but we should accept that this perspective does face questions and challenges, as will be made clear in Chapter 4.

DISAGREE

In disagreeing with this statement you might feel that context of any sort is irrelevant to the reading of a text; or, you might feel that it is particularly the contexts of genre or authorship that are not relevant (and that including (say) historical detail in your reading is much more desirable). If it is the latter, ask yourself what it is about the contexts of genre and authorship that you have a difficulty with – can you see no ways in which it would be useful to consider these?

(6)   'English literature' is a term that should refer to work by 'great' writers

such as Shakespeare: AGREE/DISAGREE/DON'T KNOW. **If you agree move down one square, if you disagree move up one square, if you don't know remain in the same position on the line graph.**

AGREE

The question as to 'what is literature?' is a commonplace of most university 'English' degrees. At the very least you are likely to come across a lecture or two on the subject. Indeed, there is a whole section dedicated to this question in Chapter 6. And if you believe that there is something called 'literature', and that this is 'greater' than other kinds of writing, ok. But spend some time thinking about what you see as the key differences between the two and, looking at a range of texts, see if your definition holds up under scrutiny. And be aware that this is a deeply political call; at certain points in history people have burned books that they didn't want others to read, and although we may live in more placid times, the question as to what gets read and taught is still an important one. It helps define what we think of as *culture*, it can even prescribe certain values and moral codes, therein affecting how we perceive the world around us and how we participate in it.

Which is a roundabout way of saying that if you agreed with this statement then you have just made a political statement about the nature of writing, culture, aesthetics, etc. – you may be surprised to realize this, but you have. The issue of a 'canon' of texts that are taught and read as (to quote Matthew Arnold) 'the best that has been said and thought in the world', is fundamentally concerned with matters of morality, politics, society, and culture.

DISAGREE

If you disagreed with the statement but you're generally quite happy with the notion of a chosen 'canon' as long as your favourite authors are in it, that is one thing. You are not objecting to or rejecting the notion of a canon in itself, but you are rejecting the idea of studying or being made to study certain writers and works. On the other hand, if you disagreed because the whole notion of a prescribed 'canon' is objectionable to you, this means you have begun to think beyond traditional ideas of what 'literature', and more broadly *culture*, is.

(7)   When interpreting a text it is impossible to ignore issues such as ethnicity and gender: AGREE/DISAGREE/DON'T KNOW. **If you agree move right one square, if you disagree move one square left, if you don't know remain in the same position on the line graph.**

AGREE or DISAGREE

This statement is complex: it has implications for the role of the author, the background of readers and the inherent qualities of the text itself. There are issues as to whether or not language, form and content can embody an ethnic or gender perspective. Because for some critics there is a particular language, voice, form, set of issues, that indicates aspects of the identity of a writer; the idea of *écriture féminine* (drawn from French feminism) for example, implies that the use of language can be gendered. For other critics it is possible to identify texts in terms of other aspects of human identity, such as 'black' or 'queer' writing.

This statement also relates to the question as to whether it is possible for any of us (writers, readers) to escape aspects of our identity, whether in fact our gender, class, ethnicity, etc. impact upon everything we do. Furthermore, there is the issue as to which of these elements of our identity have the *greatest* impact on how we think, develop and behave? Which part of our own identity most defines us? Ask yourself: when I read, am I conscious of being: (i) of a particular racial/ethnic group?; (ii) of a particular gender? (iii) of a particular social class?; (iv) of a particular sexuality? In just asking yourself these questions you are engaging in the process of becoming a more self-conscious, self-aware reader.

(8)   Genre fiction (such as romance and crime fiction) is not as well written as the classics: AGREE/DISAGREE/DON'T KNOW. **If you agree move down one square, if you disagree move one square up, if you don't know remain in the same position on the line graph.**

AGREE

If you agreed with this statement, ask yourself which texts you had in mind when you made this judgement. Think about what you judge 'good' writing to be and try to define it. This definition may well change as time progresses (and almost certainly will by the time you reach the end of this book) but it is still worthwhile to establish what you think at this point. To agree with this statement is to (hopefully) show a wide knowledge of a range of texts, but at the same time reveal a quite traditional perspective about the relative merits of different works. It may also suggest you think that there are different 'types' of reading, which can (often) be caricatured as 'beach/airport' reading versus 'intellectual/classroom' reading.

DISAGREE

If you disagreed, it is very likely that you had specific texts in mind when you made your judgement. The idea of rejecting tradition and the canon might also reveal an attempt to question inherited definitions of what is 'good' or not when it comes to literature and culture.

(9)   The critical reading of a text should focus mostly on the patterns of language and symbolism: AGREE/DISAGREE/DON'T KNOW. **If you**

agree move one square left, if you disagree move one square right, if you don't know remain in the same position on the line graph.

AGREE

Agreement with this statement suggests an initial sympathy with the broad critical methodology of 'close reading'. Close reading is concerned with the detailed consideration of the characteristics of the text 'in itself', worrying less about its various contexts (social, political, cultural, etc.). These contexts are not excluded from consideration, necessarily, but they are pushed into the background. The dominant idea is that we can learn most of what we need to learn about a text by working closely with its language.

DISAGREE

If you disagreed with this statement then by implication you are recognizing that it is important for you to consider a text's various contexts in your critical interpretation. Perhaps for you the words need to be enlightened by a wider knowledge of (say) history, genre, biography, or philosophy. Just make sure that, if context is important to you, you still give due emphasis to the words on the page.

(10) Reading and interpreting literary texts is a critical, not a creative, activity: AGREE/DISAGREE/DON'T KNOW. **If you agree move down one square, if you disagree move up one square, if you don't know remain in the same position on the line graph.**

AGREE or DISAGREE

The development of Creative Writing as a subject in universities over the last decade or so has prompted people to think again about the relationship between critical interpretation and creative expression. The modern stereotype separates the critical from the creative and embodies this in the idea of the right side of the brain (creative) versus the left side of the brain (critical). But increasingly this has been called into question. One of the emphases of *How to Read Texts* is on encouraging undergraduate students and tutors to ensure that the question of creativity in criticism is confronted as part of the process of developing your reading skills. Whether you agreed or disagreed with the statement above the key thing is that you understand the implications of your answer.

Where am I?: a critical profile

On the basis of your responses to the ten statements above you will end up at a particular position on the line graph. The position you end up at will indicate your present state of mind with regard to texts and the processes of critical inter-pretation, indicating (to an extent) what kind of reader you are at present:

How to Read Texts

(a)   If you ended up in the **north-east** quartile of the graph your tendency is towards reading texts in a non-traditional way (challenging inherited ideas about literature, culture, the canon, etc.) and you favour contextual reading, looking at the text most commonly through history, genre, biography, rather than focusing as much on its language and construction. The extent of your commitment to both of these (non-tradition/contextual reading) depends on how far up/to the right of the line graph you find yourself.

(b)   If you ended up in the **south-east** quartile of the graph your tendency is towards reading texts in a traditional way (not challenging inherited ideas about literature, culture, the canon, etc.) and you favour contextual reading, looking at the text through history, genre and biography, rather than focusing as much on its language and construction. The extent of your commitment to both of these (tradition/contextual reading) depends on how far down/to the right of the line graph you find yourself.

(c)   If you ended up in the **south-west** quartile of the graph your tendency is towards reading texts in a traditional way (not challenging inherited ideas about literature, culture, the canon, etc.) and you favour close reading, focusing specifically on the language and construction of the text rather than on its various contexts, such as history, genre and biography. The extent of your commitment to both of these (tradition/ close reading) depends on how far down/to the left of the line graph you find yourself.

(d)   If you ended up in the **north-west** quartile of the graph, your tendency is towards reading texts in a non-traditional way (challenging inherited ideas about literature, culture, the canon, etc.) and you favour close reading, looking at the text most commonly through its language and construction, being less concerned with its many contexts, such as history, genre and biography. The extent of your commitment to both of these (non-tradition/close reading) depends on how far up/to the left of the line graph you find yourself.

If you find yourself ending up at the point where you began, then your answers have to a large extent contradicted themselves, which may indicate that you have yet to come to firm conclusions on any of the key issues raised in the statements to which you responded. If you find yourself on the y (vertical) axis, then you are neither (as yet) clearly a close reader nor a contextual reader. If you find yourself on the x (horizontal) axis, then you have traditional views on certain aspects of the reading of texts, and non-traditional views on others.

That said, placing yourself on this graph is not intended to be a restrictive or restricting exercise. There is something rather interesting, I would say, if someone has a fluidity in terms of their critical positions and approaches, if they are able to utilize different methods and approaches in different situations, or in relation to particular texts, and inhabit a variety of interpretive spaces. There is nothing to say that we should all have an identifiable position and stick with it, so if you find yourself adopting specific methods for specific circumstances, that is fine. The whole point of the questionnaire and graph is merely to draw your attention to some of the implications of ideas you might have about texts and how to read them, and to try and give these implications some sort of framework as you move forward and learn more about the art and practices of reading.

Thus, the questionnaire is intended to be broadly indicative rather than an absolute definition of your critical preferences and positions; the best we can hope for is a general flavour of where you are at the present time. But wherever you end up, the point is that you put down a marker in the process of asking yourself some difficult questions about how you read at the moment, and better understand some of the presumptions you presently have about how to read texts.

As a matter of interest, keep a record of your answers and where you ended up on the line graph, so that when you repeat the exercise at the end of this book you will have a point of comparison. This need not necessarily indicate a hard-and-fast evolution from one position to another, but it might well give you some sense of the flexibility possible in your approaches to reading.

The next chapter will start the process of identifying a broader critical context for your own reading preferences. It will be concerned not just with ideas of criticism, but also with how these relate to notions of creativity and creative expression. It will illustrate ways in which criticism and creativity can work together, and in doing so can provide a more varied and imaginative engagement with texts of all kinds.

Suggested further reading

Adler, M. J. and van Doren, C., *How to Read a Book* (1972) – a highly practical guide to some of the basics of comprehending texts in a more effective and sophisticated way.

Eagleton, T., *Ideology: An Introduction* (1991) – a challenging but wide-ranging discussion of one of the 'buzzwords' of twentieth-century criticism.

Freeden, M., *Ideology: A Very Short Introduction* (2003) – a more user-friendly, but inevitably less comprehensive study of the same.

Jacobs, R., *A Beginner's Guide to Critical Reading* (2001) – contains a significant number of commentaries on a range of texts appropriate to early undergraduate level.

Spufford, F., *The Child That Books Built* (2003) – a personal account of the ways in which reading and texts play a part in individual development.

The creative critic

2

Chapter summary

This chapter will consider how the reading of texts can be approached
creatively, with students viewing their critical development and their creative
thinking (and writing) as complementary. By looking at how a range of past
writers and critics have attempted to understand the connections between
their own creative and critical practice, and ultimately by examining how
creative expression and interpretation can have a place within the critical
examination of texts, the chapter will suggest that a creative-critical approach
offers the greatest potential. This will be exemplified with specific reference to
Edgar Allan Poe's short story 'The Tell-Tale Heart'. (1841). (This is included as
Appendix A.)

Thinking about ... creativity and criticism

To begin your own process of considering ideas of 'creativity' and 'criticism',
spend some time thinking about the extent to which the following extract can
be considered 'creative' and/or 'critical'.

> What he liked about these books was their sense of plenitude and
> economy. In the good mystery there is nothing wasted, no sentence,
> no word that is not significant. And even if it is not significant, it has
> the potential to be so – which amounts to the same thing. The world
> of the book comes to life, seething with possibilities, with secrets and
> contradictions. Since everything seen or said, even the slightest, most
> trivial thing, can bear a connection to the outcome of the story, noth-
> ing must be overlooked. Everything becomes essence; the centre of the
> book shifts with each event that propels it forward. The centre, then,
> is everywhere, and no circumference can be drawn until the book has
> come to its end.
>
> (from Paul Auster, *The New York Trilogy*, 'City of Glass' (1987))

Why are we talking about creativity in a book about reading?

The discussion of criticism and creativity in this chapter is intended to provide a context for your own attempts to find a creative and original critical voice. For at the heart of *How to Read Texts* is the idea that understanding and developing your own creativity will make you a better reader, and that (reciprocally) becoming a better reader will enhance your ability to think and even write creatively. The book does not follow the more traditional and widely held view that our critical selves are separate from our creative selves. Instead it attempts to further the idea that there is a necessary, inevitable relationship between our critical and creative selves, something that is key if you are to most effectively develop your voice as reader and critic.

Different types of reader: critic vs. writer

The issue of creativity in reading is often part of a discussion of the differences between how critics read and how writers read. This tends to be seen in the competing terms of 'reading as a critic' and 'reading as a writer'. The implied distinction here is between the interrogation and examination of texts in order to understand their meaning, on the one hand, and the appreciation of texts in terms of how readers can improve their own writing, on the other. This distinction has become important as part of the development of creative writing as a university subject, one of the key means of distinguishing its approach to texts from that of English studies. So, 'reading as a writer' is not about the text itself so much as it is about what the reader can learn from the way in which the text is written, so as to develop and improve their own writing. It suggests the type of critical reading defined by Sir Philip Sidney:

> my meaning ... is not to take upon me to teach poets how they should do, but only, finding myself sick among the rest, to show some one or two spots of the common infection grown among the most part of writers, that, acknowledging ourselves somewhat awry, we may bend to the right use both of matter and manner: whereto our language giveth us great occasion, being indeed capable of any excellent exercising of it.[1]

For some critics, the difference between 'reading as a critic' and 'reading as a writer' also implies something more about the depth of the reading, with critic-readers looking for hidden or difficult meanings, working beneath the 'surface' of the text, and writer-readers working at the surface level, offering an interpretation that is closer to that of the 'general' reader who is not an academic or studying on a university course.[2] When you are being critical (so the story goes), what you do is dig deep, work hard, sweat and toil, etc. This suggests that when you are reading in a less academic fashion, you don't need to worry too much about all that stuff (and you certainly don't need to dig deep, work hard, sweat and toil, etc.), because you are only dealing with the surface of the text: the characterization, the narrative voice, the dominant patterns of imagery, the use of setting, etc. The assumption is that this is much easier, more straightforward, and almost by implication more *pleasurable* than the method of reading adopted by the critic.

....

Thinking about ... reading and pleasure

To what extent do you believe that reading should be 'pleasurable'? How would you define 'pleasurable' reading?

....

However, although the idea of 'reading as a writer' might imply a form of reading with a less explicit method or coherent approach, with no apparent critical bias or political or ideological dimension, readers should be in little doubt that it is indeed a method, with its own critical assumptions and biases. What many people call 'reading as a writer' is not dissimilar to the close-reading approaches to texts that were popular in universities during the early mid twentieth century (to be discussed at greater length in Chapter 3). The concentration on the text in terms of language, structure, parallels, symbolism, etc., advocating less of a need for specialized understanding of context or genre and the 'scholarly' dimensions of the text, is common to both 'reading as a writer' and close-reading approaches such as practical and New Criticism.

Criticism and critical theory

The distinction between 'reading as a writer' and 'reading as a critic' is also part of the aftermath of the critical-theoretical developments within literary studies during the later decades of the twentieth century, commonly known as 'critical theory' (to be discussed at greater length in Chapter 6). The prominence of philosophical critical approaches such as psychoanalysis, post-structuralism and various examples of politically aware theory (Marxism, feminism, post-colonialism, etc.) marked out the critical approaches of modern literary criticism as inescapably *different* from the sort of approaches to reading favoured by non-critics. The predominance of such philosophical-theoretical approaches to texts encouraged some readers to believe that modern criticism, with its alter-native vocabulary and sophisticated methodology, was incompatible with their own concerns and favoured approaches.

And yet, there are many examples of ways in which the division between 'what is said' (for many, the critics' sphere) and 'how it is said' (the writers' sphere) can be bridged; criticism within which the apparently *natural* separation between the way writers (as creative artists) read and the way critics (as commentators/ analysers) read is clearly not natural at all. For, there *need not* be any difference between the way critics examine texts and the way that writers who are wishing to develop and improve their own craft consider them. The social, cultural, political and economic contexts of writing, questions of authorship, critical methods, the role of the reader, concerns for form, style, pattern and structure, voice, sound, diction, tone and point of view, are relevant to all types of readers, regardless of their aspirations and motivations.

Once we accept this truth, the separation between critical and creative reading starts to break down, with all readers able to maximize their engagement with a text by combining their interpretation of 'what is said' with an equal and parallel consideration of 'how it is said' and 'why it is said'. Such an integrated approach is as fascinated by underlying messages, allegories, symbolisms, as it is with the implications of writerly choices as to point-of-view, narrative voice, showing and telling,[3] and the relationship between plot and story. This is exactly the approach of the reader confident in their own ability to offer imaginative, insightful interpretations of texts; in other words, this is the creative-critical reader.

Creativity and criticism

So, the impetus of this book is to encourage students to develop their own critical-creative voices. In particular, *How to Read Texts* is an encouragement to break down barriers between the critic and the creative writer/artist, many of which seem to have become more apparent over recent decades. And there is plenty of evidence to suggest that these barriers are artificial – criticism from the earliest times has shown the potential for creative exploration. Critics have experimented with form and content, producing dialogues (Plato, John Dryden), verse criticism (Horace, Alexander Pope), critical letters (John Keats), critical essays (Matthew Arnold, W. H. Auden), and critical treatises (Sidney, Percy Bysshe Shelley). More recently, 'ficto-critics' have developed a combination of imaginative writing and literary criticism within single texts, linking textual features such as formal conventions, characterization and plot, to a consideration of salient critical issues and debates.

Creativity and criticism: some past ideas

It is also true to say that there have been numerous examples of past critics and writers who have offered their own thoughts as to the nature of the relationship between the critic and the writer:

The artist is king

For many, the talent of the artist has been seen as clearly superior to the skill of the critic. Note, for example, the thrust of the criticism of Samuel Johnson (1709–84), who was both a writer and a critic:

> we owe few of the rules of writing to the acuteness of critics, who have generally no other merit than that having read the works of great authors with attention, they have observed the arrangement of their matter, or the graces of their expression, and then expected honor and reverence for precepts which they never could have invented: so that practice has introduced rules, rather than rules have directed practice.[4]

For Johnson, criticism was the inferior form because it contained nothing that was in itself original, and it was viewed almost as if it were a parasite feeding off the texts of great authors.

This was a view shared by Johnson's contemporary Alexander Pope (1688–1744), who wrote that only those who could 'themselves excel' should be allowed to 'teach others',[5] by commenting on the strengths and weaknesses of texts. The role of the critic was not insignificant for Pope, but it was important that professional critics kept in mind the extent of their all too obvious limitations:

> But you who seek to give and merit fame,
> And justly bear a critic's noble name,
> Be sure yourself and your own reach to know,
> How far your genius, taste, and learning go;
> Launch not beyond your depth, but be discreet,
> And mark that point where sense and dullness meet. (p. 37)

If a critic was to be truly great (and successful), this self-awareness was vital:

> Be silent always, when you doubt your sense;
> And speak, though sure, with seeming diffidence:
> Some positive, persisting fops we know,
> Who, if once wrong, will needs be always so;
> But you, with pleasure own your errors past,
> And make each day a critique on the last. (p. 51)

The critics had roles as 'modern [a]pothecaries ... by doctor's bills to play the doctor's part' (p. 39); in diagnosing the ailments of poetry. However, it had to be recognized that they did not have the artistic sense themselves. Further, 'Poetry' was just one of the 'nameless graces which no methods teach, and which a master-hand alone can reach' (p. 40); it was a form beyond the reach of men dominated by their critical senses.

Percy Bysshe Shelley (1792–1822) took the idea of the superiority of creative work above criticism yet further, categorizing the writing of poetry as a different kind of activity from the measured, intellectual process of criticizing: 'Poetry ... is not subject to the control of the active powers of the mind ... its birth and recurrence have no necessary connection with consciousness or will.'[6] For Shelley, there was a separation between the rational, conscious mind and the creative, unconscious instincts that were inherent in the poet's being. The poet's 'power', his 'intervals of inspiration', were evident when he was 'abandoned to the sudden reflex of the influences under which others habitually live' (p. 296). The artist had to lose control of their critical judgement in order to be able to create their best work; but it was exactly this sense of control that the critic had to maintain if he was to fulfil his own role effectively.

Thinking about ... poetry

In the extract above, Percy Shelley focuses specifically on 'poetry'. How is poetry distinct and different from other forms of writing?

A creative/critical balance

The Roman critic Horace (65–8 BC) was one of the first to argue that the artistry of the writer had a positive connection with their critical abilities: the reader 'must have nothing to do with any poem that has not been trimmed into shape by many a day's toil and much rubbing out, and corrected down to the smallest detail.'[7] Artistic inspiration and an artisan's labour were for him combined to fashion the literary text into a coherent whole, and without this critical element the text would not succeed. There had to be a 'friendly compact' between 'application' and 'a strong natural aptitude', of 'native genius ... [that] is cultivated' (p. 93). The innate creative power of a writer could only achieve its full potential if the writer was able to apply themselves critically to their task, selecting the most effective language, understanding the rules of form, and editing the text into a coherent shape.

This more equal relationship between criticism and creative work was also apparent in the much later artistic philosophy of Samuel Taylor Coleridge (1772–1834). Coleridge suggested (notably in *Biographia Literaria* (1817)) that there was no inherent separation between the creative and the critical faculties: 'this power, first put into action by the will and understanding, and retained under their irremissive, though gentle and unnoticed ... controul [sic]'.[8] There was for him instead an ongoing, positive link between each faculty: 'GOOD

SENSE is the BODY of poetic genius, FANCY its drapery, MOTION its LIFE, and IMAGINATION the SOUL that is everywhere, and in each; and forms all into one graceful and intelligent whole' (p. 185). So, when Coleridge discussed poetic metre he saw this as a way in which artistic creativity and a critical appreciation of form could combine, a 'supervening act of the will and judgement, consciously and for the foreseen purpose of pleasure' (p. 219). The inspiration of the artist was managed and controlled by the restrictions of form, which were themselves enforced through the critical judgement of that artist.

Henry James (1843–1916) was much disillusioned by the state of criticism during his own age: 'there is such a flood of precepts and so few examples – so much preaching, advising, rebuking and reviling, and so little *doing*: so many gentlemen sitting down to dispose in half an hour of what a few have spent months and years in producing'. For him, a 'single positive attempt, even with great faults, is worth generally most of the comments and amendments to it'.[9] And yet, James also recognized that the extent and nature of critical debate was a vital element in the creation of great art:

> Art lives upon discussion, upon experiment, upon curiosity, upon variety of attempt, upon the exchange of views and the comparison of standpoints; and there is a presumption that those times when no one has anything particular to say about it, and has no reason to give for practice or preference, though they may be times of honour, are not times of development – are times, possibly even of a little of dullness. The successful application of any art is a delightful spectacle, but the theory too is interesting; and though there is a great deal of the latter without the former I suspect there has never been a genuine success that has not had a latent core of conviction. Discussion, suggestion, formulation, these things are fertilizing when they are frank and sincere.[10]

Interaction between criticism and creativity was thus not just important, but an essential element of a healthy culture, within which 'ones sees the critic as the real helper of the artist, a torch-bearing outrider, the interpreter, the brother'.[11]

This was closer to T. S. Eliot's (1888–1965) view of criticism and art as mutually supporting, although in Eliot's case this mutual support was focused upon the work of the artist/critic: 'the nearest we get to pure literary criticism is the criticism of artists writing about their own art', in that 'the criticism of artists writing about their own art is of greater intensity, and carries more authority'.[12] For Eliot there was a level of insight, of direct personal experience, at the heart of what an artist/writer did that made anything they had to say about texts and how they operated more apposite and perceptive. Thus, for him the division between writer and critic was overcome, although only *truly* for those who were practising *both* forms of expression.

Thinking about ... criticism and writing

Eliot argues that the best critics are writers. Make the case both for and against this proposition.

So is it possible to be critical and creative at the same time?

Yes. And the case has been well made in the past. Take Oscar Wilde, for example, who argued strenuously that 'the highest Criticism ... is more creative', and that without 'the critical faculty ... there is no artistic creation at all worthy of the name'.[13] For Wilde, criticism was 'in itself an art ... really creative in the highest sense of the word ... both creative and independent' (p. 965). It was in a very literal sense original, producing something new out of pre-existing materials (texts), and not even requiring 'the finest materials' (p. 966) at that; it was possible, he argued, to create a masterpiece of critical reading which focused on a text that was poorly written and constructed. This meant, for Wilde, that criticism was 'in its way more creative than creation', having 'least reference to any standard external to itself', and providing 'its own reason for existing' (p. 966).

Creative criticism

This sense of the potential creativity of criticism is important, for it allows readers to break down some of the apparent barriers between writers and critics. It helps the appreciation of the way in which there is something graceful, lyrical, moving even, about a great piece of critical writing. Critical writing can stimulate and excite, and make you sit forward on the edge of your seat with a strong sense of being confronted with material delivered in an imaginative way, just as fiction or poetry or drama can. If you read criticism that has this effect then you are conscious of the way it stirs your thoughts, and forces you to consider things in new ways. This is just what criticism *should* do.

The following extracts are drawn from much longer works of criticism that had just such a profound effect on me:

Franco Moretti, *The Atlas of the European Novel* (1998)

An atlas of the novel. Behind these words, lies a very simple idea: that geography is not an inert container, is not a box where cultural history 'happens', but an active force, that pervades the literary field and shapes it in depth. Making the connection between geography and literature explicit, then – mapping it: because a map is precisely that, a connection made visible – will allow us to see some significant relationships that have so far escaped us.

> Such a literary geography, however, can refer to two very different things. It may indicate the study *of space in literature*; or else, *of literature in space*. In the first case, the dominant is a fictional one ... in the second case, it is real historical space .... The two spaces may occasionally (and interestingly) overlap, but they are essentially different ... [14]

What is interesting about the opening to Moretti's book is the sheer energy of his prose and the ideas it is attempting to encapsulate. There is a real sense of new ideas being created out of the conjunction of more familiar ones, and of a new intellectual territory being (literally and metaphorically) 'mapped out'. The denial of geography as a symbolic 'container', to be replaced by something more dynamic and 'cultural' and active is a major statement of intent, providing for the interaction between geography and literary study that characterizes the book as a whole. The ideas and their expression are wonderfully creative, imagining alternative ways of thinking and presenting them in colourful and dynamic language.

> Thomas Carlyle, *Sartor Resartus* (1833)
>
> Considering our present advanced state of culture, and how the Torch of Science has now been brandished and borne about, with more or less effect, for five thousand years and upwards; how, in these times especially, not only the Torch still burns, and perhaps more fiercely than ever, but innumerable Rush-lights and Sulphur-matches, kindled thereat, are also glancing in every direction, so that not the smallest cranny or doghole in Nature or Art can remain unilluminated, – it might strike the reflective mind with some surprise that hitherto little or nothing of a fundamental character, whether in the way of Philosophy or History, has been written on the subject of Clothes.[15]

Carlyle's use of grandiose language and extravagant statements and metaphors is characteristic of his writing more generally, and he became famous (or notorious, depending on whether you appreciate his work or not) in the nineteenth century for the elaborate and dramatic way in which he wrote criticism, history and philosophy. What the reader is confronted with in this extract is an intellectual mind passionately engaged in the process of creating its own way of seeing and thinking, and Carlyle can be seen as one of the most creative thinkers of his time. In terms of the language he uses, his notion of the 'innumerable Rush-lights and Sulphur-matches, kindled thereat ... glancing in every direction, so that not the smallest cranny or doghole in Nature or Art can remain unilluminated' is literary, imaginative and deeply poetic.

But it is also Carlyle's ideas, just as was the case with Moretti, that are creative. His philosophy of the 'clothes', the outward manifestations of identity and the way humans live, that must be 'read' for what they can tell us about people and society, amounted to a theory of signs more than a century before theorists such as Roland Barthes (1915–80) and Umberto Eco (1932–), in texts such as *Mythologies* (1957) and *A Theory of Semiotics* (1976), were key figures in the modern development of *semiotics*. Rooted in Ferdinand de Saussure's (1857–1913) conception of the relationship between the *signifier* and the *signified* (the interlinked pair that make up every *sign*), semiotics became one of the most influential and wide-ranging critical approaches of the twentieth century, a powerful method of accounting for how meaning is conveyed through language and identifying how a culture connotes its own value system through the everyday aspects of social life.

The idea, put at its most straightforward, and clearly delineated in the Carlyle text as a whole, is that everything around us is a *sign*; it indicates, suggests, connotes, denotes (whatever term you wish to choose) *meaning*. Just as road or street signs attempt to tell us something about how we must drive, the direction we must take, or the location of landmarks or obstructions, so it is also possible to read the clothes people wear (using the Carlylean metaphor), their body language, their accent, the nature of where they live/work/spend time, etc., as indicators of underlying meaning about what they think/believe/value. Thus, each of these 'signs' is made up of a *signifier* (the jumper I wear, the house I live in) and a *signified* (whether I am a follower or setter of trends, whether I am affluent or poverty stricken, etc.). And for semioticians this is how it is possible to 'read' the underlying nature of society or, more specifically, for *How to Read Texts*, how it is possible to understand written texts – by decoding the word-signs they are made up of. Carlyle *anticipated* this explosion of interest in cultural signs and how they operate, and his artistic imagining of how this might work illustrates effectively just how *creative* criticism can be.

CONSIDER:

In semiotic theory, 'signs' are all around us. Identify three signs (from books, TV, film, etc.) and analyse how they work/what they mean.

Criticism as creativity/creativity as criticism

The point to remember is that these pieces of writing (the Moretti and the Carlyle) are in their own ways just as creative as any examples of fiction or poetry or drama that you might care to cite. They toy with language and ideas, they imagine aspects of the world in ways previously unimagined, and they display an artistic means of conjuring up the colours and textures of texts and cultures. Such works illustrate why and how creative writing and criticism are closely related. The complexity and sophistication of ideas can be similar, and the engagement with critical questions comparable, even if the method or means of representing them is different. Think, for example, of a work such as John Fowles's *The French Lieutenant's Woman* (1969), a novel as critically sophisticated as any piece of criticism you could find. Moreover, not only is it critically sophisticated, it *knows it is*; it makes a great display of it; it prides itself on its critical engagement with a range of issues and literary debates. In other words, *it shows off*. There is a level of self-assured display that makes the reader sit up and take notice.

> **(1)** I do not know. This story I am telling is all imagination. These characters I create never existed outside my own mind. If I have pretended until now to know my characters' minds and innermost thoughts, it is because I am writing in (just as I have assumed some of the vocabulary and 'voice' of) a convention universally accepted at the time of my story: that the novelist stands next to God. He may not know all, yet he tries to pretend that he does. But I live in the age of Alain Robbe-Grillet and Roland Barthes; if this is a novel, it cannot be a novel in the modern sense of the word.[16]

This wonderfully playful confession of authorial fallibility connects the narrative of the novel with later twentieth-century debates about the role (indeed the 'death') of the author, and the role of the sort of omniscient narrator that was often found in Victorian fiction (of which Fowles's novel is a partial critique/ parody). The extract is critically informed within the context of the ongoing fictional story.

> **(2)** For a while his travelling companion took no notice of the sleeping Charles. But as the chin sank deeper and deeper – Charles had taken the precaution of removing his hat – the prophet-bearded man began to stare at him, safe in the knowledge that *his* curiosity would *not* be surprised. (p. 347)

Taken out of context this passage may appear unremarkable. However, once the reader becomes aware that in fact this 'travelling companion' is in reality Fowles (the author) himself, who has stepped into the narrative of his own novel to achieve a close inspection of his lead character, it becomes apparent that (following on from the earlier quotation from the novel) the whole notion of the author, growing out of the work of critics such as Roland Barthes, is up for grabs. Fowles is providing a creative illustration of the extent to which this is the case, blurring the line between author and character, fiction and reality.

> **(3)** For I have returned, albeit deviously, to my original principle: that there is
> no intervening god beyond whatever can be seen, in that way, in the first
> epigraph to this chapter; thus only life as we have, within our hazard-given
> abilities, made it ourselves, life as Marx defined it – *the actions of men* (and
> of women) *in pursuit of their ends.* (p. 398)

This extract brings the reader full circle; the so-called 'realist' novel that is the
foundation of *The French Lieutenant's Woman* is undermined by the claim that
the narrator knows much less than the reader might expect. The novel makes the
point also made at much greater length by Barthes in his essay 'The Death of the
Author' (to be discussed at length in Chapter 4), that the authority of the author
must always be questioned.

The French Lieutenant's Woman is a novel that is as much about the critical
debates surrounding the nature of the novel and authorship as it is about the
lives of the fictional characters of Charles Smithson, Ernestina Freeman and
Sarah Woodruff. The text has (for example) three different endings, each of
which is critiqued by the narrator and then left for the reader's own consideration. The novel questions the very nature of storytelling, the status of the author
(as authority), and displays an ongoing (though entirely playful) disregard for
the more familiar aspects of the novel form. It forces the reader to think about
their own reading practices, the nature of 'the text' and the status of 'reality'. The
text as a whole is a serious exploration of critical issues within the confines of
what purports to be a realist novel.

Thinking about ... metafiction

The critical 'label' often applied to texts such as *The French Lieutenant's Woman*
is 'metafiction', a term denoting fictional works that explicitly engage with
critical debates about the nature of fiction. What do you think writers might be
trying to achieve in writing metafictional texts?

Critical/creative reading: Edgar Allan Poe, 'The Tell-Tale Heart'

The final section of this chapter is a demonstration of how a reader might
develop a creative-critical reading method. It is based on the ideas of 'reading as
a critic' and 'reading as a writer' referred to earlier in this chapter, and it attempts
to show how these two apparently different reading strategies, one rooted in
a critical concern with establishing meaning, the other in a writerly concern

with reading as a means of improving creative practice, can come together and produce a multi-layered, sensitive and critically informed understanding of a text. The readings will focus on Edgar Allan Poe's 'The Tell-Tale Heart' (the full text of which can be found in Appendix A).

And the critic says ...

When looking at Poe's story with the eye of a stereotypical critic, we might wish to consider its depths and hidden meanings, and the particular symbolism used. For instance, we might be concerned with the nature of the *heart* at the centre of the tale. The heart that beats so loudly, in the perception of the murderer who is also the narrator, that it eventually destabilizes him mentally and precipitates the final-act confession of guilt. Quite what does this heart truly represent, we might ask? What is it that, beneath the surface (literally) of the narrative (it is buried under the floorboards, after all) that the narrator is so scared of? How come the implied presence of the old man who has been murdered (in the form of his dismembered body) has this effect on him? Furthermore, what was it in the first place about the man (beyond 'his eye': 'he had the eye of a vulture – a pale blue eye, with a film over it'[17]) that led the narrator to kill him?

Now, the critic who is looking for deeper textual meaning might see this fear, anxiety and overwhelming mental fragility as an indicator of some form of repression. The narrator, after all, says right at the beginning of the story that: 'I loved the old man' (p. 277). So, what if (and we need not become obsessively Freudian for this interpretation to start to work) this repression is actually sexual? What if in fact the neurosis of the male narrator about the all-seeing eye of the old man, a neurosis that leads to extreme paranoia and then murder, is rooted in a terror that the old man 'knows' about some particular aspect of the narrator's sexuality that he wishes to keep secret? Perhaps it's a sign of some deep sexual longings that the narrator would much rather remain buried, and this results in the murder of the old man (the man who 'knows'), with his body being 'buried' (along with the narrator's secret). If we pursue this reading, we could see the nagging beat of the disembodied heart that terrorizes the narrator as a recognition of the fact that, even though the old man is now gone, the secret lives on, demanding to be revealed. The end paragraph, in which the narrator then confesses all to the awaiting policemen as a means of purging himself of the secret that will not be silenced, can be seen as a figurative or symbolic 'coming out' to the world, in the form of a confession of murder (which, necessarily, will lead to the uncovering of the secret as well).

This 'critical' reading of the story, in terms of decoding its hidden meanings, could be explored to a much greater extent. For instance, the specific nature of the narrator's sexual anxiety could be considered, and this might be read through the lens of (say) Freud's theories of human sexuality, or else queer theory. What is important, however, is that the reading is all the while striving to uncover textual meaning; not the ways in which the text works, the devices it uses, or the writerly choices Poe made so as to best achieve his desired effect, but what it might *mean*.

And the writer says ...

One of the central aspects of the Poe short story that might be of interest to our writer-readers, who are reading (let us not forget) as a means of learning how to improve their own writing rather than necessarily in order to establish textual meaning, is the way in which the narrative point-of-view is achieved. This is a key aspect of what was earlier called the *surface* of the text. And it is through this point-of-view that Poe achieves the almost psychotic immediacy of the story, wherein the reader is sucked in to the frenzied ramblings of a murderer, invited to unpick the inconsistencies of the events that are unfolding. This starts right at the beginning: 'TRUE! – nervous – very, very dreadfully nervous I had been and am; but why *will* you say that I am mad?' (p. 277). The effect of this direct (second person) address is intended to be disconcerting and destabilizing. It challenges the reader as if they belong to the wider world that is set against the narrator. The sense of paranoia is tangible: 'How, then, am I mad?' (p. 277) the narrator asks us.

Throughout the story Poe skilfully utilizes the narrative point-of-view to conjure up the confrontation and confusion that is itself a metaphor for the belligerent and at times bewildered mind of the murderer: 'I was never kinder to the old man than during the whole week before I killed him' (p. 277). This becomes more apparent as the plot unfolds: 'I knew it was the groan of mortal terror. It was not a groan of pain or of grief – oh, no! it was the low stifled sound that arises from the bottom of the soul when overcharged with awe. I knew the sound well' (p. 278). This disturbed narrator's voice shows rather than tells the reader about his mental state (how does he know these things?), hinting at a troubled life beyond the frame of the narrative. And because we as readers learn through this 'showing', rather than being told by an omniscient narrator, we instinctively imagine the worst.

The language Poe uses takes the reader on a tour of a diseased psychology: 'I knew what the old man felt, and pitied him, although I chuckled at heart' (p. 279). It is the repeated and continual switch between direct second-person address to the reader ('you cannot imagine' (p. 279)), more orthodox first-person narration ('when I had waited a long time' (p. 279)), and non-specific, non-directed address ('Almighty God! – no, no!' (p. 281)) that creates the effect of multiple voices speaking simultaneously, offering the reader a narration of multiple personalities.

This outline reading of 'The Tell-Tale Heart' could be the starting point for a more lengthy, detailed 'writerly' consideration of the text. It offers a close examination of some of the language and devices within the story that Poe uses to create his desired effects, and it has the potential to help developing writers improve their own writing, through the close consideration of writing technique.

And the creative-critical reader says ...

Both of these readings have strengths and weaknesses. The supposedly 'critical' reading strives to decode the Poe short story and offers an interesting explanation of the underlying meaning of the tale. The 'writerly' reading, on the other hand, pays much more specific attention to the language of the story itself, and is sensitive to the writerly craft behind the effects of disorientation and confusion that are the story's key strengths.

But neither of these readings is entirely satisfactory on its own. The former, though more intellectually intriguing than the latter, lacks specific textual reference, and doesn't get to grips with the words on the page(s) quite enough. The latter, though more detailed and specific, lacks a world-view, a means by which to make all the individual points and comments contribute towards an overarching sense or interpretation. Interestingly, each of the readings is lacking in exactly what the other is strong in; the former lacks detail but has an overview, the latter lacks an overview but has detail.

Much better, one might argue, to configure a way of reading the text that bridges the gap between the two; a reading wherein the writerly choices the author has made are placed within the context of the overarching quest to understand the text's meaning, with both elements complementing and therein strengthening each other. Which could lead us to feel that there is something unnecessarily artificial about the separation between 'writerly' and 'critical' readings, just as there is between what we define as our 'critical' and our 'creative' sides. And, in terms of how this impacts upon your development as an undergraduate reader of texts, this could be the difference between an imaginative and groundbreaking reading, and an orthodox and unremarkable one.

Intervening in texts

Towards the end of the twentieth century a theory of reading emerged that has rich potential for bridging the gap between the creative and the critical. It has not as yet been widely adopted on university courses in the UK or US, perhaps unsurprisingly, but as the barriers between creative work and critical work come down there is every chance that it may do. It is called 'textual intervention'.[18] The idea is that readers 'intervene' in texts, as a means of developing their own interpretative/reading skills. The specific form of this 'intervention' can vary, but it usually involves the reader altering or extending the original text in some way. Once this has been done, the reader reflects on the implications of what they have done, and in doing so they sharpen their own understanding and appreciation of the original text. Through this process of intervention and reflection, the reader learns about literary form, style and genre, while at the same time understanding more about the meanings and nuances of the original text. Playing with the text broadens and strengthens the reader's capacity to read and interpret it: 'The best way to understand how a text works … is to change it: to play around with it, to intervene in it in some way (large or small), and then to try to account for the exact effect of what you have done' (p. 1).

This notion of critical and creative exploration in unison offers an interesting and potentially powerful way of bringing text and criticism to life at once:

> you will constantly and with every tool at your disposal – critical, analytical, theoretical and historical – be forced back into it [the original text]. Every turning you take, every choice and combination you make will be gauged against one already taken and made in your base text. (p. 2)

In the case of the Poe story, one potentially valuable 'intervention' would be to re-imagine and rewrite the story as if the narrator was female. In that context, we might consider how the language might take on different significances: 'I was never kinder to the old man than during the whole week before I killed him' (p. 277). Does the emphasis and impact of this alter if the speaker is a woman? In considering the disturbed mental state of the narrator we might ask whether this is amplified or qualified by a change of gender? Sentences such as 'I knew what the old man felt, and pitied him, although I chuckled at heart' (p. 279) could perhaps be seen as taking on a more menacing air.

The gendering of the narrator might also be important in considering the symbolic significance of the heart in relation to illicit sexual desire (as in the earlier critic's reading of the tale). The connotations of 'I loved the old man' (p. 277) change with a female speaker, and it is rather more difficult to sustain a reading of the story that implies that the wish to hide illicit sexual desire or behaviour was the motivation for the murder.

In reflecting on the differences between this 'new' version of the story with a female narrator and the original, the reader's attention is drawn to how heavily gendered the narrative voice is in the original Poe story. This is a realization that is facilitated through the creative intervention. So, the effect of the intervention is in fact to further the critical understanding of the story, reinforcing the point that critical and creative skills are most effectively developed in parallel rather than in opposition.

Checkpoint 1

This is the point to test your understanding of the ideas discussed in this chapter:

- What is creative criticism? Try and identify specific examples of criticism that you think are creative.

- When you are *criticizing* a text as part of your degree course how different does this process *feel* to when you are reading a text 'for pleasure'?
- What do you understand by the term 'art'? Do you think that criticism can be art? Why/why not?
- Create your own 'intervention' into 'The Tell-Tale Heart', imagining the different story that would result if you made one or two key changes to the original. Contrast the two versions of the story (Poe's and your own), thinking all the while about how your reading of the original has been enhanced by this creative-critical process.

Suggested further reading

On theories of criticism/creativity

Coleridge, S. T., *Biographia Literaria* (1817) – an important landmark in the process of combining philosophy and criticism.

Eliot, T. S., 'To Criticize the Critic' (1965) – one of many seminal critical essays by Eliot.

Freud, S., 'Creative Writers and Day-Dreaming' (1908) – a consideration of the subconscious elements of human creativity.

Horace, 'On the Art of Poetry' (18 BC) – an early example of criticism on poetic form.

James, H., 'The Art of Fiction' (1884) – examines the relationship between fiction and reality.

Koestler, A., *The Act of Creation* (1964) – considers the nature of creativity.

Pope, A., 'An Essay on Criticism' (1711) – a lengthy verse criticism by a key eighteenth-century writer/critic.

Pope, R., *Textual Intervention: Critical and Creative Strategies for Literary Studies* (1995) – defines a new method for creative/critical engagement.

—— *Creativity: Theory, History, Practice* (2005) – a study of creativity in its various forms since the earliest times.

Shelley, P. B., 'A Defence of Poetry' (1821) – an influential battle cry about the social importance of poetry and poets.

Sidney, Sir P., *A Defence of Poetry* (1595) – a significant statement of Renaissance criticism.

Wilde, O., 'The Critic as Artist' (1891) – advocates the creativity and artistry of the critic in his own right.

Wordsworth, W., 'Preface' to *Lyrical Ballads* (1798) – the groundbreaking definition of Romantic creativity and sensibility.

On reading as a writer:

Brande, D., *Becoming A Writer* (1934) – pre-theoretical ideas of writing and reading.

Lubbock, P., *The Craft of Fiction* (1921) – early 20th century thoughts on the writing craft.

Other relevant critical/creative works:

Barthes, R., *Mythologies* (1957) – a semiotics key-text.

—— *Elements of Semiology* (1964) – likewise.

Carlyle, T., *Sartor Resartus* (1833) – philosophy and literary experimentation rolled into one.

Eco, U., *A Theory of Semiotics* (1976) – another defining text of semiotics.

Hawkes, T., *Structuralism and Semiotics* (1977) – a clear and effective guide to the above.

Stepping things up

Once you have completed all the exercises in this chapter, and feel comfortable that you have absorbed the ideas, perspectives and approaches it has discussed, you are ready to engage in some more challenging work:

(1) Consider how different ideas of 'creativity' are represented in 'The Man with the Twisted Lip'. (This story can be found in Appendix C)

(2) To what extent can 'The Man with the Twisted Lip' be seen as a criticism of later nineteenth-century English society?

(3) In what ways are 'signs' important in the unfolding of the story of 'The Man with the Twisted Lip'?

Close reading

Chapter summary

This chapter introduces 'close reading' through a short history of some close reading methods, looking at how close reading skills have been more or less prominent at particular points of literary-critical history. Key strengths and weaknesses of close reading approaches will be discussed, which will include examining the political and philosophical assumptions that have underpinned various types of close reading. The chapter will conclude with a creative and critical exploration of close-reading methods with specific reference to William Blake's poem 'The Tyger' (1794) (this is included as Appendix B).

Thinking about ... close reading

To begin your own process of considering how close reading works as a method of textual criticism, spend some time thinking about exactly how much you can find to say about the following extract. (To support your 'reading' you should refer to nothing outside of/beyond the extract itself.)

> HENRY VIII, the unconquered King of England, a prince adorned with all the virtues that become a great monarch, having some differences of no small consequence with Charles, the most serene Prince of Castile, sent me into Flanders, as his ambassador, for treating and composing matters between them. I was colleague and companion to that incomparable man Cuthbert Tonstal, whom the King with such universal applause lately made Master of the Rolls, but of whom I will say nothing; not because I fear that the testimony of a friend will be suspected, but rather because his learning and virtues are too great for me to do them justice, and so well known that they need not my commendations unless I would, according to the proverb, 'Show the sun with a lanthorn.' (from Sir Thomas More, *Utopia*, Chapter 1 (1516))

What is close reading?

Close reading is the detailed and specific interpretation of a text through its language, considering the prevalent images, symbols, metaphors and patterns it incorporates. It is an attentive form of reading, often limited to short works or excerpts of longer texts; lengthy texts *can* be read in this way in their entirety, although it should be acknowledged at the outset that the intensity of work that close reading demands could make this a very time-consuming process! Close reading can lead to extremely detailed and lengthy critical expositions based on even the most scant of materials (let alone whole novels). To take an extreme example, Jacques Derrida's essay 'Ulysses' gramophone'[1] takes up more than 80 pages focusing solely on the meanings of the word 'yes' in James Joyce's novel *Ulysses* (1922).

As an initial illustration of how close reading works and differs from other critical approaches, it is worth briefly considering how close readers might begin to look at a specific text. So, in looking at T. S. Eliot's 'The Love Song of J. Alfred Prufrock' (1917), a typical close reader might begin their process of exploration by examining the way in which the poem scans in particular extracts, as part of the wider structure/framework of the poem:

> When the evening is spread out against the sky
> Like a patient etherised upon a table;
> Let us go, through half-deserted streets,
> The muttering retreats

and consider the way the metaphor of the patient 'spread out' like the evening flows into the tight rhyming pattern of 'streets' and 'retreats'. This might progress into considering the specific use of language sounds as the poem moves into its well-known refrain about the women who 'come and go ... talking of Michelangelo'. There appears to be an inherent contrast or even tension here between the ordinary women and this great man of renaissance art, one that is designed to operate dramatically and ironically. The close reader would, however, tend not to place the poem within the context of early-twentieth-century modernism, or attempt to relate the bleakness of the poem to the anxiety and gloom engendered by the Great War (1914–18). Neither would they be likely to tease out a reading of the poem wherein Prufrock was seen as Eliot himself within a verse-autobiography, in which moments in the poem were specifically related to the unfolding of Eliot's actual life.

The key thing to remember, with close reading, is that everything begins with the text. The emphasis of the criticism, the analysis of the words on the page, all starts (and often ends) with those words. The close reader is less interested (in some cases uninterested) in questions as to how the text relates to its literary context, or in any other contextual debates to do with culture, politics and society.

As such, close readers work up a reading of the text through a tight focus on the specific details of language, often with no reference at all to anything beyond the text (e.g. the life of the author, the politics of the time of publication, its place in literary history). Instead the reader/critic attempts to explain the text and the way it works, as a kind of internal structure, through its diction (choice of words), syntax (construction of the sentences), tone (attitude or voice of the narrator/speaker), and *internal* context (how selected sections relate to or illuminate the work as a whole).

The idea of texts as self-contained structures was partly influenced by the development of structuralist philosophies in the earlier twentieth century, although structuralist criticism and close reading are not to be confused. For there were a range of critics writing before the twentieth century who also shared the view of texts as autonomous structures. Alexander Pope, for example, talked of how the critic should judge the 'joint force and full result of all' rather than 'the exactness of peculiar parts'.[2] Therein, the *structure* of the text was deemed as significant: 'the whole at once is bold and regular' (p. 43). Such thinking anticipated the way in which close readers became interested in the ways in which texts set up their own patterns, doubles and echoes within the context of a coherent whole.

One of the seminal texts on the way in which language was part of such a structure was Ferdinand de Saussure's *Course in General Linguistics* (1916). Saussure wrote about how language worked to convey meaning through difference and opposition i.e. because the language we use (termed 'parole') was part of an overarching structure, with a supposedly limited amount of words (termed 'langue'), it was possible to establish what a single word meant by contrasting it with all the words it *was not*. So, for example, the word 'table' could be seen as denoting an actual table only because it did not refer to a 'chair' (because there was a word for that already), just as it did not refer to a 'house', 'dog', 'banana', or anything else because *there were other words that referred to these things*. Within this framework of language, words were seen as arbitrary; there was no inherent or inevitable reason that the physical object we recognize as a 'table' should actually be called 'table', for example. The word only had this meaning because there was an overarching structure of language within which every word had its place. Our 'parole' (language/speech) had meaning because the 'langue' provided clear boundaries and a fixed range of possibilities.

....

Thinking about ... words and meanings

For Saussure, there was no particular reason why a word and its meaning were connected – the connection between (say) the word 'sky' and the actual sky was arbitrary. Select five words and consider whether the relationship between word and meaning ('signifier' and 'signified') appears to be arbitrary, or whether there might be some inherent connection between the two.

....

A history of close reading

Close reading has had, for a number of years now, something of a negative reputation in universities. There have been contemporary critics who have advocated the close-reading cause, such as James Gribble in *Literary Education: A Re-evaluation* (1983) and George Watson in *The Certainty of Literature: Essays in Polemic* (1989), but more generally the view in literary-critical circles has been that close reading is not only something to do with the past, but to do with the bad old times when prejudice in literary criticism was allowed to go unchecked, and when the social and moral chauvinisms of critics were rife. It is only recently that those involved in the teaching of English at university level have felt comfortable enough to return to talking about the possibility of close reading without anticipating uproar. Nevertheless, the idea that close reading might be part of the future of textual criticism rather than the past, let alone being one of the central planks of English studies,[3] is still very contentious.

The reasons for close reading being viewed by literary critics as a poor relation to the developments in theoretical-philosophical criticism of the 1980s and 1990s are various. But a key part of the reason for this was that many close reading critics were also *liberal humanists*; liberal humanism being a broad philosophy that assumes a universal core to human experience, and in many cases stretching this universal core to include aesthetics and aesthetic judgements, which are seen as non-political and not related to different cultural contexts. So, for example, the high value placed on the works of Shakespeare could, within this liberal humanist mindset, be seen as a fixed, ahistorical judgement, one for all cultures (of the past, present and future). Liberal humanism also privileges the role of the human individual in the creation of art and culture, rather than the society and culture from which they emerged, inevitably leading to rather less of a stress on the significance and impact of history.

The link between close reading and liberal humanism meant that as the latter became increasingly challenged from the middle of the twentieth century, until the point that for many it became identified as an outmoded view of the world, close reading was tarnished by association. Just as liberal humanism became seen by some as past its sell-by date, so close reading was judged likewise. And as literary criticism became increasingly (in an overt sense) 'political' towards the end of the twentieth century, the rejection of and attacks on liberal humanism (and at the same time close reading) became more and more virulent.

Thinking about ... universalism

Do you believe that there are aspects of human existence that are 'universal'? Does this include judgements about the value and quality of certain texts?

Origins

Just because close reading has been seen by many modern critics as old-fashioned, this should not lead undergraduate students to ignore it. For it has been very prevalent at different points in our literary-critical history, and there is evidence of aspects of a close reading method as far back as the criticism of Aristotle. For him, every tragedy was seen to contain six main elements, 'plot, character, diction, thought, spectacle, and song.'[4] Of these, 'the most important' was 'the plot' (p. 39). The effect of this close consideration of the formal elements of tragedy put his work into the area of what we might now call *formalist* criticism, but the methods deployed (detailed consideration of language, character, narrative, etc.) identifies a method that is not dissimilar to close reading. Aristotle did not leave things there, however; he combined his close consideration of the text with a consideration of how audiences responded emotionally to the formal and performative elements of tragedy. Therein his focus switched to the relationship between text and audience (a.k.a. reader).

This close consideration of the text also has some connection with the work of another Greek critic, Longinus, who noted how in the highest writing there 'are five particularly fruitful sources of the grand style ... the ability to form grand conceptions ... the stimulus of powerful and inspired emotion ... the proper formation of the two types of figure [thought and speech] ... the creation of a noble diction ... [and] the total effect resulting from dignity and elevation.'[5] The method by which the critic was supposed to establish each of these aspects was a close reading one; the detailed study of the text in order to establish the connections between language, form and the achievement of artistic effect.

Yet, despite the fact that close reading has such historical origins, it was not until the twentieth century that it became the pre-eminent method of textual study, a pre-eminence that continued for many decades. Key in this development was I. A. Richards, who developed a reading approach known as Practical Criticism, wherein the words of the text themselves were the primary, indeed sole object of study. This idea of 'practical criticism' first emerged in the work of Samuel Taylor Coleridge, who wrote about how: 'In the application of these principles to purposes of practical criticism as employed in the appraisal of works more or less imperfect, I have endeavoured to discover what the qualities in a poem are.'[6] And for Richards, the specifics of the text had to be analysed in order to move towards a more scientific method that could be understood by other readers and taught to students; his was a reaction against what he saw as the more speculative critical approaches followed by many of his antecedents and contemporaries. Richards's *Principles of Literary Criticism* (1924) and *Practical Criticism* (1929) were important texts in establishing his critical doctrine in the UK, and anticipating the New Criticism of the 1930s and 1940s in the US.

Richards was one of the first English tutors at the University of Cambridge, and his influence on the discipline of English studies, as the pioneer of this form of textual study, was enormous. Not only was his 'school' of critical approach fashionable for many years, but he was also one of a number of critics who served as the chief point of contrast for the developments of critical theory during the 1980s and 1990s. These were decades when 'close reading', 'practical criticism' and 'new criticism' became terms of insult and disparagement.

Practical Criticism, Richards's most famous text, begins by identifying the different stages of reading of a poem: 'first must come the difficulty of *making out the plain sense* [original italics] of poetry',[7] before moving through the 'difficulties of *sensuous apprehension*', 'the place of *imagery*' (p. 14), the 'powerful very pervasive influence of *mnemonic irrelevances*' [the reader's transference], then '*stock responses*' (p 15), '*sentimentality*', '*inhibition*', '*doctrinal adhesions*', '*technical presuppositions*' (p. 16), and then finally '*general critical preconceptions*' (p. 17). Richards regarded the four aspects of human utterances to be 'sense' [an intention to say something], 'feeling' [emotional responses to the subject matter], 'tone' [the attitude towards the listener], and 'intention' [the effect being promoted or conjured up] (p. 181).

The intention of Richards's critical approach was to ensure that 'something can be done to make men's spiritual heritage more available and more operative' (p. 309). Close reading was about opening up subject matters to new, uninitiated readers. Reading poetry successfully was 'a craft, in the sense that mathematics, cooking, and shoemaking are crafts' (p. 312). This practical-critical approach wasn't concerned with the influence of literary tradition, placing the focus solely on the text itself: 'Far more than we like to admit, we take a hint for our response from the poet's reputation. Whether we assent or dissent, the traditional view runs through our response like the wire upon which a climbing plant is trained' (p. 316). There was also an inherent suspicion of so-called psychological criticism: 'Poetry has suffered too much already from those who are merely looking for something to investigate and those who wish to exercise some cherished theory' (p. 322). Richards did not argue that psychology had no place in literary criticism, rather that it needed to be accommodated within the scientific framework of close reading:

> [between the] two extreme wings of the psychological forces there is the comparatively neglected and unheard-of middle body, the cautious, traditional, academic, semi-philosophical psychologists who have been profiting from the vigorous manoeuvres of the advanced wings and are now much more ready than they were twenty years ago to take a hand in the application of the science. (p. 322)

Interestingly, much of the late twentieth-century backlash against Richards's work, within which he came to be seen as an arch-conservative with a method that preserved rather than challenged tradition, belied the actual content of his works. This is most apparent in *How to Read a Page* (1943), which is more open to both contextual and generally alternative readings than is usually acknowledged of Richards's work: 'we may reasonably doubt whether there is one right and only right reading ... different minds have found such different things in them that we would be very rash if we assumed that some one way of reading them which commends itself to us is the right one'.[8] This suggests that in practice close reading was less dogmatic than has often been claimed, allowing the possibility of analysing 'how the varied and possible meanings hang together, which of them depend upon what else, how and why the meanings which matter most to us form a part of our world – seeing thereby more clearly what our world is and what we are who are building it to live in' (p. 13).

For Richards, the reason for focusing on the text itself, rather than any of its contexts, was straightforward:

> Modern historical scholarship especially terrorizes us with the suggestion that somewhere in the jungle of evidence there is something we happen not to know which would make the point clear, which would show us just what the author did in fact mean. That suspicion of a missing clue is paralyzing – unless we remember firmly that from the very nature of the case essential clues are always missing. However much evidence we amass, we still have to jump to our conclusions. Reading is not detection as the perfect detective practises it. We are never concerned with facts pointing conclusively to a central fact – what happened in an author's mind at a given moment. No facts could ever establish that. If psychoanalysis has done nothing else for the world it has at least helped us to realize that minds – including the authors' minds – are private. All we can ever prove by factual evidence is *an act* – that the author wrote such and such words. But what he meant by them is another matter. (p. 14)

Readers were not to concern themselves with what 'was going on in the author's mind when he penned the sentence', and, instead with 'what the words – given the rest of the language – may mean' (p. 15). But this was not so much because Richards wanted to fossilize one particular meaning of the text (an accusation often levelled at close reading), but in truth because for him there was nothing that the reader could be certain of other than the words. Contexts (biographical, social, political) had to be excluded from consideration because of the impossibility of the reader ever truly knowing about these things to a reliable extent. As such, the close focus on textual language was not an ideological decision, based on a narrow philosophy or restrictive method, but rather a pragmatic one – based on the fact that Richards did not have confidence that a reader could establish the context of a text in a meaningful, usable way.

Thinking about ... reading and knowledge

Are there things about texts that it is not feasible for a reader to know for sure? If yes, what are they?

The New Criticism

The New Criticism was the name of the critical perspective that became commonplace in the US in the 1930s and 1940s, and which became prominent, predominant even, in Western textual study for much of the remainder of the twentieth century. The name of this approach was taken from John Crowe Ransom's *The New Criticism* (1941), which was one of the key texts in the rise of New Criticism across universities and schools across the US and beyond. As with Richards's 'practical criticism', New Criticism tended to avoid discussing a text in relation to the author, their intentions and biography, or the contexts from which the text emerged. Indeed, critics such as W. K. Wimsatt and M. C. Beardsley criticized the 'intentional fallacy' wherein the author's own intentions were seen as a key aspect of the analysis of a text, and the 'affective fallacy', where the effect of the text on the reader was viewed as key.[9] The prescribed critical method of the New Critics was to view the text as a self-contained structure, a web of words, symbols and images. Texts existed in their own right, and didn't need additional or extraneous information to enlighten them. The text was the creation of a particular author, but the circumstances of this author were not allowed to be taken into account when interpreting the narrative/poem/play. Individual works were thus seen in isolation from any sociological or biographical detail by which they could be 'read'. New Criticism was very much a practical method of reading rather than a philosophy of interpretation.

The New Criticism opens by stating that the 'most fundamental pattern of criticism' was 'criticism of the structural properties of poetry'.[10] This view was typical of close reading approaches, as has been seen. Ransom then went on to identify what he saw as the weaknesses evident in other forms of criticism, which included a reliance on 'the idea of using the psychological affective vocabulary in the hope of making literary judgements in terms of the feelings, emotions, and attitudes of poems instead of in terms of their objects' (p. xi), as well as a tendency for some criticism to fall into what he called 'plain moralism' (p. xi).

As was the case with Practical Criticism, the reputation of New Criticism declined significantly towards the end of the twentieth century. New Criticism became an Aunt Sally to be attacked and ultimately knocked down, viewed as the enemy of literary-critical progress. And yet, as with the work of I. A. Richards, many examples of New Criticism were in truth less narrow and restrictive in their focus on the text than they have often been accused of being. For instance, Ransom's objection to psychology and moralism came not because he saw such considerations as *irrelevant* to the analysis of a poem; the chapters of *The New Criticism* focus specifically on the way in which key critics (I. A. Richards, T. S. Eliot and Yvor Winters) look outside the text itself as part of their readings: praising the work of 'the psychological critic', 'the historical critic' and 'the logical critic' respectively. Thus, there is no sense at all that these extra-textual matters are extraneous or unimportant.

And this is reiterated when Ransom discusses the work of Richards specifically, wherein he delineates the five 'contexts' of poetry: physiological, psychological, biological-psychological, biological-logical and aesthetic. These show New Criticism viewing literature in relation to a range of contexts, far from being hostile to contextual approaches. The consideration of poems in relation to the neural responses they generate, the intellectual responses engendered, and the ways in which texts negotiate between readers and their societies and interact with other forms of literary expression, are *all* contextual.[11] Indeed, Ransom goes on to celebrate T. S. Eliot precisely *because of* his use of external materials and knowledge in his readings of poems: 'It is Eliot who uses his historical studies for the sake of literary understanding, and therefore might be called a historical critic' (p. 139).

For Ransom, historical critics 'know the threads of factual and intellectual history which connect some English poet with the incidents of his own life, with the "thought" and "interests" of his age, and with contemporary and earlier poets in the same "school" or "tradition"' (p. 138). This latter aspect, the role of literary context or 'tradition', was most applicable to Eliot:

> But what occurs to him most characteristically, and most makes him the powerful critic he is, is that it can never cease to be instructive to see a poem in the light of other comparable poems; and perhaps that a critic's fertility derives from his power and patience to observe the limits within which the like poems differentiate themselves and branch off from each other. (p. 141)

But what was key for New Criticism was not so much whether critical analysis looked at text or context, but more whether theoretical or dogmatical approaches were adopted: 'Eliot has nothing like a formula ready in advance; he looks at the poem against its nearest background to see what sort of criticism it needs; he comes up presently with a set of judgements which are comparative in the first instance, but critical in the end' (p. 141). Context *could* be examined as part of the 'New Criticism', but only on the basis of the pragmatic judgement of the critic that this was necessary in the specific case of the text they were looking at, at any one time.

That said, it must be acknowledged that there were other New Critics who were less prone to considering contexts within their reading of texts. Cleanth Brooks, in his *The Well Wrought Urn* (1949), for example: 'If literary history has not been emphasized in the pages that follow, it is not because I discount its importance, or because I have failed to take it into account. It is rather that I have been anxious to see what residuum, if any, is left after we have referred the poem to its cultural matrix.'[12] Brooks wanted to move beyond seeing the poetry of the past as merely 'cultural anthropology' and poetry of the present as merely 'political, or religious, or moral instrument' (p. vi). What was crucial for him was what was 'inside' the poem, the detail of its structure and formation and imagery and symbolism. To summarize its contents or list its constituent parts was a crude gesture that he called 'the heresy of paraphrase' (p. 164); his conviction was that 'the poetry must be wrested from the context' (p. 175) and examined in terms of its internal details.

Yet, even for Brooks, 'to stress the poet is, of course, a perfectly valid procedure' (p. ix). It was acceptable to consider 'his ideas, his historical conditioning, his theories of composition, and the background, general and personal, which underlies his work' (p. x). It was also appropriate at times 'to stress the response of the reader to a poem and to consider the nature of that response as the poem makes its impact on various kinds of people and upon various generations' (p. x). What the New Critics thus seemed to be striving for was a sophisticated critical layering within which many different strands and levels of critical engagement could co-exist: the status of the author, the significance of the reader(s) and the processes of reading, the nature of the text and its own role within the construction of meaning, were *all* potential areas of exploration *alongside* the tight and focused concentration on the language of the text itself.

As such, the New Critical position (articulated by critics such as Brooks) should be seen as less restrictive than has often been claimed. New Criticism juxtaposed a close reading method: 'there is something to be said for concentrating on the poem itself as a construct, with its own organization and its own logic', with a recognition that there were other factors to consider at the same time: '[poems] ... do not grow like cabbages, nor are they put together by computers ... They are written by human beings ... [and] remain mere potentialities until they are realized by some reader.' It was seen as the role of every critic to 'realize that he is a reader, and an imperfect reader at that, with his own blind sides, prejudices and hasty misreadings' (p. x). This acknowledgement of the partial, inherently political nature of all reading/criticism illustrates how New Criticism was in fact open, rather than closed, to alternative critical interpretations and practices, an image far from the caricature of narrow-mindedness and political naivety that close reading was confined to during the 'theory' years of the later twentieth century.

Thinking about ... close reading and form

Why do you think that so many of the critics who deployed 'close reading' techniques chose poetry, rather than fiction, as their subject matter?

F. R. Leavis

F. R. Leavis was one of the most high-profile and influential critics of the mid-twentieth century, utilizing a close-reading-type method within the context of his broader consideration of the ways in which texts upheld particular moral values and codes of behaviour. Leavis looked to texts to 'teach' readers about life and human nature. He advocated the study of those texts that best suited this overarching moral purpose. Hence, in his *The Great Tradition* he talked of a 'canon' of the English novel form which enshrined the artistic and creative abilities of specific authors, whilst at the same time praising their moral seriousness and weight. 'Literature' was therein seen as having a beneficial social impact, affecting the morals, feelings and intellects of readers in positive ways. Clearly influenced by T. S. Eliot, Leavis saw 'great' writers as part of a literary *tradition*:

> Jane Austen, in her indebtedness to others, provides an exceptionally illuminating study of the nature of originality, and she exemplifies beautifully the relations of 'the individual talent' to tradition. If the influences bearing on her hadn't comprised something fairly to be called tradition she couldn't have found herself and her true direction; but her relation to tradition is a creative one.[13]

For him, Austen did not merely passively inherit the tradition within which she worked, she adapted conventions and expectations and left a legacy for novelists who followed her, which could then be added to by them.

Central to this was Austen's moral dimension: 'without her intense moral preoccupation she wouldn't have been a great novelist' (p. 7). Crucially, within the context of a close reading, this was allied to great technical skill: 'The great novelists in that tradition are all very much concerned with "form"; they are all very original technically, having turned their genius to the working out of their own appropriate methods and procedures' (p. 7). Morality was thus embodied in form and technique, with the writer's skill shown in how they matched each to the other in the most appropriate fashion. This was why, in part, Dickens (who Leavis was happy to concede was 'a great genius and is permanently among the classics' (p. 19)) was not placed within this 'great tradition'. For his genius was seen as that 'of a great entertainer ... [someone who] had for the most part no profounder responsibility as a creative artist that this description suggests' (p. 19). The lack of moral thought in his work meant that 'the adult mind doesn't as a rule find in Dickens a challenge to an unusual and sustained seriousness' (p. 19).

This moral dimension of Leavis's criticism was one of the central reasons his work fell out of favour towards the latter end of the twentieth century. Such moral judgements within the context of textual analysis came to be seen as inappropriate, politically questionable even. Yet, despite this, and the fact that Leavis's name came to be widely disparaged within literary criticism, it would be a mistake to overlook the fact that in viewing the twentieth century as a whole his impact on the study of texts was as great as that of almost any other single critic of the period.

Thinking about ... value judgements

Are there some writers whose work you judge to be better than that of others? What standards of judgement are you using in answering this question?

Other forms of close reading

Elements of close reading were central to a number of other critical developments and approaches in the twentieth century:

Stylistics

Stylistics defined itself as the scientific and objective study of texts, using what was seen as textual data and employing its own terminology. Stylistics concerned itself with the similarities between *ordinary* language use and that used in so-called *literary* texts. It tried to show that there were no meaningful differences between the two, and that 'literary' did not equal 'special'. Each text was considered as a whole, for the effects it achieved and the language it used to do so. Stylistic critics used specialized terms drawn from the science of linguistics to define their findings. This was often harder to understand than the usual non-jargonistic language of close reading (which could be academic, but was not scientific) and consequently stylistics was often seen as a more specialized, technical method of literary criticism. This technical quality was evident in the work of critics such as Roman Jakobson (1896–1982).

Stylistics was rooted in the idea that texts could be objectively understood, and that they had a single 'truth' to tell. Any notion that texts had qualities (e.g. aesthetics) that were beyond clear scientific definition was rejected. Having said that, one of the complexities of stylistics was that despite its claims to the contrary, it did offer interpretations of texts rather than simply scientific analyses. It may have used so-called 'scientific' data to support its speculative, subjective conclusions, but they were speculative and subjective nevertheless. So, whereas judgements to do with the syllabic make-up of words could be seen by stylistic critics as objective, the purposes to which they put such 'scientific' judgements, such as in considering the effect of writing in relation to its implied reader(s), were interpretive and debatable.

Russian Formalism

Another form of critical approach that relied on elements of close reading, although within the context of a broader consideration of the literary qualities of texts in relation to other texts, was Russian Formalism. This was one of the most influential schools of critical thought in the twentieth century, having a relationship with other literary-critical developments such as structuralist criticism and stylistics. Russian Formalism emerged out of Russia in the early decades of the twentieth century, and a number of critics adhered to its broad critical philosophy, including (illustrating the interlinking of different perspectives) Roman Jakobson. The key for the Russian Formalists, as with the New Critics, was that texts were to be judged in themselves, to be the subject matter of criticism largely in isolation. They felt that their more scientific approach (with literary works seen as 'machines'), ignoring psychology or history or culture as contributing factors to the production of textual meaning, made for a more coherent sense of literary criticism, preventing any blurring between literary study and other disciplines such as history, psychology, anthropology and sociology.

The key thing for the Russian Formalists was that 'literature' was distinctly different from any other aspect of human culture, and it was treated as such. The focus was on the words rather than any philosophical or ideological contexts. 'Poetic language' was defined and was the sole object of study. The Russian Formalists were content to acknowledge that texts were the product of authors and their intentional activity, they just didn't see this as the point – once the text (the 'machine') had been created, it then existed autonomously.

Yet, despite their claims to the contrary, the Russian-Formalist approach had fundamental political implications. For instance, there was the idea that there was a necessary and clear distinction between art and non-art. This was in itself a reaction against the dominant view in Russia during the earlier twentieth century that texts were inevitable aspects of political and social history. The Russian Formalists thought that 'literature' was more 'special' than that, that the language used in literary texts (as art) should be celebrated. Their particular area of interest was the language of poetry, and how the sounds of words related to the understanding of what was literary and what was not. Poetic language was seen to have an identity and character of its own, with literary criticism a method of identifying this. Key, in this discussion, was the concept of 'defamiliarization' (*ostraneniye*). Poetic language had the capability to defamiliarize the reader, to show old things in new ways, casting fresh light on the world and human experience. The defamiliarizing language of poetry (in particular) distinguished it from more ordinary, denotative forms of language.

Yet, despite the apparent focus of Russian Formalism being solely on the text-in-itself, with an accompanying reluctance to view the text as the cultural/political voice of the author, the issue of context was fundamental to how the Russian Formalists defined literature. For the whole notion of 'defamiliarization' was based on the contrast between the poetic and the unpoetic, art and non-art. The text worked on the reader by estranging them, by presenting its subject matter in a way that drew attention to itself by using language in a way that was not 'ordinary', not 'normal'. So in a work such as T. S. Eliot's poem *The Waste Land* (1922) the reader was defamiliarized with the colloquial refrain 'Hurry up please it's time' within the context of a poem that was highly literary and allusive. The simple words 'Hurry up please it's time' became literary themselves because of their apparent contrast with the surrounding frame of reference. But the reader only recognized this defamiliarization if they understood the poem's *context*. The identification of what was poetic language was entirely reliant on a continual referrence to the literary and linguistic context beyond it. Poetic language only became poetic language when the reader understood its place within the context of non-poetic language; art was only art when there was a clear and coherent sense of what was *not art*. Thus, in Russian Formalist criticism the context was *integral* to the appreciation of the text itself.

Further close readings

There has tended to be an assumption in many accounts of the development of twentieth-century criticism that close reading was something that critics 'got over' on their way towards more sophisticated, often more explicitly politically aware approaches to reading. Thus there is an anticipated opposition between (say) Marxism and close reading, or feminism and close reading, or post-colonial theory and close reading. However, such an account of the history of literary criticism in the twentieth century is in truth barely half of the story. For some of the philosophical-critical approaches of the later-twentieth century still utilized a broad 'close reading' method, even if their aims and objectives were somewhat different from the close readers of the earlier century. A particular case in point is *deconstruction*, the literary-critical exemplification of post-structuralist philosophy, originated by Jacques Derrida (1930–2004).

Deconstruction was fundamentally concerned with the ways in which meaning was 'constructed' by writers, texts and readers, and the key role language had within this process. It placed particular emphasis on unpicking the ideas, assumptions, prejudices and ideologies, either hidden or explicit, within texts. This was made more problematic by the fact that, on its own admission, deconstruction denied coherent senses of meaning and truth, so that in the process of considering how texts operated, it was also questioning the ability to 'know' anything. It was as if deconstruction was, by its very nature, arguing itself out of existence. When pressed, even Derrida himself was seemingly unable to clearly define what deconstruction was, stating that: 'I have no simple and formalizable answer to this question.'

Nevertheless, in all the labyrinthine arguments about what deconstruction was/was not, one thing was relatively clear. For all its modern philosophical feel, and the fact that (for a long time) deconstruction was at the cutting edge of literary criticism, the broad approach to texts inherent in deconstructive criticism was akin to that adopted by orthodox close-reading critics of the past. In particular, there was an overarching concentration on the text in and of itself. For Derrida, there was 'nothing outside of the text',[14] so that was where the focus should be. And, although this was not an acceptance that there was nothing *beyond* the language of the text, the words of the text were seen to be of primary importance. Such a focus downplayed the significance of authorial biography and the relations between the text and historical context or genre conventions. It asserted a need for a detailed and specific consideration of the slipperiness of the language on the page(s).

One of the key differences between deconstruction and other versions of close reading was, however, how the method was used; whereas the close readers of the early twentieth century were looking for structures and patterns and coherent relationships between different elements of the text, deconstructionists tended to look for the opposite: imbalances, oddities, incongruities; the moments when the text contradicted itself, when there were tensions between form and content. Deconstruction was like a celebration of the impossibilities of fixed meaning and representation, drawing attention to the gaps between language and signification, a kind of exploratory feast within which the reader enthusiastically moved from one word or symbol to the next in search of critical play.

The assumptions of close reading criticism

Close reading criticism of the earlier twentieth century was reliant on a number of assumptions about texts and how to appreciate them:

- That criticism was about the text itself (with an inherent recognition that there was something identifiable as 'the text').
- Reading was about uncovering the meaning of the text, including any moral/life lessons it might convey.
- Close reading tended not to place texts in their context(s); context was often seen as irrelevant to the interpretive process, with meaning found within rather than without the text. These contexts were sometimes acknowledged as having an importance, but more often than not they were overlooked as part of the process of close reading.
- For some close reading critics textual interpretation was connected to judgements about values and morality, which were often seen as universal; great literature tended to be viewed as timeless for the way in which it enshrined these (universal) values and morals.

The benefits of close reading

The main strengths of a close reading method are that:

- It encourages the development of an eye for textual detail and an understanding of the workings of language. It could be argued that this is vital for all effective readers/critics.
- It ensures that the reader/critic becomes familiar with texts to a significant degree – if there is nothing else to consider, nothing else to bring in from the outside, then the textual reading must be worked up entirely from within.
- There is no temptation to become distracted with external (perhaps extraneous) issues, such as biography, genre, or historical context; these can (if handled clumsily) lead to a reader/critic *imposing* a reading on a text, bringing to bear their own agendas/issues and almost forcing the text to comply.
- Close reading can (its advocates would argue) lead not just to a greater appreciation and understanding of the text, but also a greater *enjoyment* of its complexities.
- Close reading tends to be less speculative than some other forms of critical engagement; the reader/critic works with what is in front of them and nothing else (and so is less likely to find themselves speculating about abstract relationships and connections).
- Close reading can be seen as more inclusive than other forms of criticism; it doesn't require any additional knowledge of context or genre and need not be concerned with scholarly allusions within a text to other texts. All readers begin with the same material to work with (the text itself). This might mean that their reading is less reliant on their knowledge/education and more on their critical skills.

The problems with close reading

Because close reading begins and ends with the text itself, often no allowance is made for external aspects such as historical context or genre conventions. The reader is not encouraged to develop a wider understanding of the relationships between the text they are studying and other texts with which it might have some kind of relationship. So, for example, we might study Monica Ali's *Brick Lane* (2003) and not consider its relationship with multiculturalism in Britain in the twenty-first century, or Salman Rushdie's *The Satanic Verses* (1988) without examining its reception across the world. These things, we might well judge, are important aspects of any appreciation of these texts. We might decide that a full appreciation of a text is not just about a rigorous grasp of the text as language.

How to Read Texts

- To exclude historical context and imply (explicitly or implicitly) that the text (the words on the page) is unchanging, is to imply that the world, values, morality, human nature, are unchanging also. If we exclude the impact and significance of historical forces on our textual readings then we ignore the potential of texts to change (e.g. offer differing interpretations over time), as well as denying the status of texts as products of social change in and of themselves. For example, viewing the plays of Shakespeare in isolation from an understanding of Elizabethan politics, wherein plays retold a favoured version of history (that reinforced the validity of the royal family line), overlooks an aspect of the texts that is of great significance. Indeed, the popular myth of the child-killing, Machiavellian _Richard III_ is the result of just such a wider political dimension of the plays, wherein Richard was represented in this way to discredit his family line and to bolster that of the reigning monarch. Ignore this fact of the play and we misread its social function within the Elizabethan context.

- As soon as critics start talking in terms of the 'enjoyment' and 'appreciation' of texts they are working with concepts that are very slippery and even contentious. These notions are inherently subjective, thus very difficult to use within critical readings because of the difficulty in conveying what is meant by them.

- Although close reading might be seen as less speculative than other critical methods, it might also be seen (perhaps consequently) as less creative as well. For it is the speculation, the hypothesizing, the (potentially) endless expansion of the text into different areas and histories, that (one might argue) makes criticism the dynamic area of literary study that it is. To limit the discussion to the words on the page could be to limit the potential of criticism, and to limit the potential subject matter the critic can refer to within any reading. Many of the more exciting, creative and groundbreaking examples of textual criticism over recent decades (such as Franco Moretti's 'literary geography' discussed in Chapter 2) have been produced precisely _because of_ critics pushing back the boundaries and opening up (not closing down) the field of study.

- Though it could certainly be argued that close reading is more inclusive than some other forms of criticism, in that it doesn't require any additional knowledge of context or genre, in practice this inclusiveness has not been evident. Close reading has (too often) been associated with a textual search not just for meaning, but for the 'right' meaning, about decoding the text and understanding what the author _really meant_. Some close reading has been about establishing the 'proper' interpretation of the text, with the implicit assumption that there is a single meaning for each text. So, rather than being _more_ inclusive, close reading has in truth been _less_ so at times, leaving readers unable to arrive at the prescribed single meaning of the text marginalized.

- The close-reading method can be extremely intensive, working through the text word-by-word, producing extraordinarily detailed readings. T. S. Eliot identified this as 'the lemon-squeezer school of criticism', whereby 'the method is to take a well-known poem ... without reference to the author or to his other work, analyse it stanza by stanza and line by line, and extract, squeeze, tease, press every drop of meaning out of it that one can'. His conclusion was that this method 'is interesting and a little confusing', and a 'very tiring way of passing the time'.[15] He rejected the notion that 'there must be just one interpretation of the poem as a whole, that must be right' (p. 113) and that the interpretation of a poem was 'necessarily an account of what the author consciously or unconsciously was trying to do' (p. 114). He felt that the method of close reading as a whole 'was as if someone had taken a machine to pieces and left me with the task of reassembling the parts' (p. 114).

Creatively exploring close reading

Whatever the decision that is made about the balance of the advantages and disadvantages of a close-reading method, it is obvious that being able to read texts in detail, and with a sensitivity to language, is a valuable skill to possess. The ability to maximize the potential of any given text to produce the most comprehensive reading is an important one. And to be able to do so is not necessarily to become one of Eliot's dreaded 'lemon squeezers'. The key is to learn the skill of discriminating between what is most valuable within a text and what is not, understanding how to prioritize the elements of our reading.

The creative exercise below is intended to help you in your efforts both to maximize critical readings of given texts and to appreciate which are the key points that need to be made. The challenge, if that is the right term, is for you to write your own short poem. It can be written in a particular short form if you wish, such as a haiku or limerick, or it can be blank or free verse. It need not be written on any particular subject, indeed the exercise works best if you don't have anything specific in mind when you write it. For the idea is that it will be open to as many different readings as possible; the language therefore can be ambiguous, not thought through, barely coherent at times (it *really* doesn't matter). The point is that the imagery and symbolism shall encourage a reader to speculate and imagine and use their own conjecture as to what is being said.

This process need not take more than half an hour. And what you produce doesn't have to be any good – don't feel inhibited by the need to produce something that is of quality (to be honest it's more fun if it's bad poetry – it works just the same and doesn't take so much time!).

Once you have produced your short poem (5–10 lines maximum), put it away for a few hours at least. When you come back to it, having given it as little thought as you can for the intervening period, your task is to provide as many different interpretations of the poem as you can possibly come up with. Concentrate very hard on the specific language of the poem, and on what the poem as a whole is achieving (or not) and how. Try to offer at least one coherent reading of the poem as a whole, as well as more specific interpretations of words and images and lines. Test yourself to see just how much material you can excavate from your *ad hoc* piece of poetry, which should then give you some indication as to how fruitful a close critical reading can be.

Critical reading: William Blake, 'The Tyger'

Following on from your work on your own 'poem', the next task is to deploy your close-reading skills in a reading of a text written by someone else, in this case 'The Tyger' by William Blake (the full text of which is to be found in Appendix B). Read the poem carefully, and more than once, before beginning your critical exploration.

The first thing you *might* have noticed about Blake's poem is that the image of the tyger (tiger) 'burning bright' that opens the poem invites the reader to consider the various potential significances of 'burning'. The most obvious interpretation is that Blake is referring to the stripes like bright, fire-like stripes across the animal. This strong orange, set against the 'forests of the night' (i.e. alluding to the blackness of the backdrop) marks an obvious contrast between darkness and light. This opposition has often been seen, historically, in terms of the opposition between good and evil. This contrast would be emphasized were we allowed to consider the symbolic opposition Blake creates between the tiger and the lamb in his *Songs of Innocence and Experience*, within which the former is seen to symbolize the modern, cruel, industrial world, and the latter is seen as the ideal, rural, pastoral world of the past. However, as we are concerned solely with the words of the poem rather than its contexts, this line of interpretation cannot be developed.

This representation of the tiger is also significant through the association between fire and danger. As it is one of the elements, this can perhaps be seen to imply a connection between the tiger and nature, and even (potentially) the evolution of the earth and the creation of species. The lines 'what immortal hand or eye/could frame thy fearful symmetry?' reinforces this, suggesting the presence of a God-figure, which ties in to the idea that the tiger itself is part of some overarching scheme of the natural world. The unorthodox, forced rhyme of 'symmetry' draws the reader's attention to the word and its meaning, and the question mark at the end of the line is rhetorical, addressed to either the reader or the world beyond.

The next stanza ('In what distant deeps' to 'sieze the fire') continues with the speculation as to the origins of the tiger, and the process by which he could have been created. The vastness of this creation and his own size are emphasized. This feeds into the use of the word 'art' in stanza three, which appears to work in a variety of ways. 'Art' suggests a contrivance or creation, but at the same time it implies an opposition with 'nature' and the natural world. The effect of this is to question the relationship between nature and art, as well as to introduce the idea of an omniscient God with the 'artistic' (i.e. creational) power to give life to creatures, just as the artist gives life to sculptures, paintings or writing.

In stanza four, Blake draws on images and language associated with industry and industrialization, a social phenomenon in its relatively early stages at the time the poem was written. 'What the hammer? what the chain?' coupled with the mentioning of 'furnace', and 'anvil' put the reader in mind of an industrial workshop, another obvious (and traditional) opposition with the natural world that is embodied in the tiger. Unfortunately, a close reading of the poem cannot continue too far down this line of interpretation without dealing with industrialization itself, which falls outside the boundaries of the close reading method.

Stanza five introduces the idea of an external 'he' who is framing and shaping the world, culminating in the line: 'Did he who made the Lamb make thee?' The impact of this line is significant. There is an inherent opposition between the lamb (innocence, religiosity, purity, whiteness) and the corruptions of the tiger (worldliness, colour, modernity). The question is about whether the two creatures could have been created by the same Being (God), but it is also about whether such a creation of opposites is even feasible, such is the profound difference between them. This links with the final stanza, which is a refrain of the first but with a twist at the end. Rather than the final line being 'Could frame thy fearful symmetry?' it has changed to 'Dare frame thy fearful symmetry?' There is a sense of challenge at the heart of the use of 'dare', questioning the role of an immortal being in the tiger's creation.

The '1794' that concludes the poem presents the close reader with a problem. Even if we might suspect, or even know, that this is the date of the poem's production or publication, this is a contextual, rather than textual, matter. This means that there is little we can say about it in isolation from the language of the poem. Perhaps we can read it as part of the rhythm of the poem (which doesn't seem likely), but otherwise we have to largely overlook it if we intend to keep rigidly to the close reading method.

This sketched outline of the poem marks out some of the aspects of the text that could be worked up into a more substantial close reading. It works with the language of the poem, considering this specifically, and it doesn't move too far into aspects of the poem that are inevitably contextual. There is obviously much more that can be said about the language and structure of the poem, the patterns and images and symbolic framework of 'The Tyger', and all of this would feature if this outline reading was developed. What we can say is that this initial sketch of a reading shows just how quickly the close-reading method can produce results. In almost no time at all paragraphs of readings have emerged that themselves offer the potential to be expanded upon into a more lengthy reading.

Checkpoint 2

At this point you should test your knowledge and understanding of the issues raised in this chapter through seminar discussion/individual reflection:

● How similar is 'close reading' to the way you have studied texts in the past (at previous levels of study)? Does it feel comfortable/natural?

● What areas/issues might you not be able consider in close reading that you would personally want to consider as part of your textual reading?

● Why do you think that some people regard close reading as old-fashioned? Make the case for close reading being both old-fashioned as well as being still relevant in modern reading and criticism.

● Choose another poem from Blake's *Songs of Innocence and Experience* and offer your own close reading of it in outline. When you have finished, list what you judge to be the strengths and weaknesses of this reading. Find another reading of the same poem from a published book of criticism and compare it with your own; what issues does this second reading touch upon that your own did not?

Suggested further reading

Brooks, C., *The Well Wrought Urn: Studies in the Structure of Poetry* (1949) – an early example of New Critical practice.

Burke, K., *Philosophy of Literary Form* (1939) – earlier-century, text-focused criticism with a New Critical flavour.

―――― *A Grammar of Motives* (1945) – more New Criticism.

Derrida, J., *Of Grammatology* (1976) – a key text of Deconstruction.

―― 'Ulysses' Gramophone: Hear Say Yes in Joyce' (1984) – a wonderful example of a close-reading method.

de Saussure, F., *Course in General Linguistics* (1916) – a foundation text for a variety of subsequent critical approaches.

Eliot, T. S., 'The Frontiers of Criticism' (1965) – another influential essay from the Eliot critical canon.

Empson, W., *Seven Types of Ambiguity* (1930) – from one of the leading proponents of close reading.

―――― *Some Version of Pastoral* (1935) – and another.

―――― *The Structure of Complex Words* (1935) – and another.

Jakobson, R., *The Framework of Language* (1980) – useful in understanding the relationship between structuralism and stylistics.

Leavis, F. R., *The Great Tradition* (1948) – much maligned, but hugely influential in terms of the nature of 'the canon'.

Ransom, J. C., *The New Criticism* (1941) – the origins of a hugely significant critical 'movement'.

Richards, I. A., *Practical Criticism: A Study of Literary Judgement* (1929) – close reading *par excellence*.

—— *How to Read a Page* (1954) – a work of close reading but also open to other critical possibilities.

Tate, A., *On the Limits of Poetry* (1948) – another work from the broad church of 'New Criticism'.

Warren, R. P. and C. Brooks, *Understanding Poetry* (1938) – written by two of the key critics in the New Critical movement.

Wellek, R. and A. Warren, *Theory of Literature* (1949) – a text clearly influenced by New Criticism but one that also looks beyond the dominance of close reading techniques towards a consideration of biography, psychology, genre, literary history, culture and the role of the reader.

Wimsatt, W. K., *The Verbal Icon: Studies in the Meaning of Poetry* (1954) – more orthodox formalist criticism, rejecting the intention of the author and the interpretation of the reader.

Wimsatt, W. K. and M. C. Beardsley, 'The Intentional Fallacy' (1954) – published both as part of the above and also (initially) as a separate essay; key in the critical rejection of authorial 'control' over textual meaning.

Winters, Y., *The Function of Criticism* (1957) – influenced by New Criticism but also highly individual in its moralism.

Stepping things up

Once you have completed all the exercises in this chapter, and feel comfortable that you have absorbed the ideas, perspectives and approaches it has discussed, you are ready to engage in some more challenging work:

(1) Select any ONE page of 'The Man with the Twisted Lip' (which can be found in Appendix C) and offer your own close reading of it.

(2) Consider the tone of the narrative voice in 'The Man with the Twisted Lip'; what specific language does Conan Doyle use to achieve this tone?

(3) Examine the ways in which 'The Man with the Twisted Lip' uses symbols, patterns and parallels as part of its narrative construction.

4

Biography and authorship

Chapter summary

This chapter will look at different ways of considering the role of the author within the process of reading texts, and will consider the benefits and risks of such approaches. The discussion will consider, among other things, the status and significance of biography, theories of authorship, and the ways an author's life can be used to help establish textual meaning. This will be illustrated through a reading of Charlotte Brontë's *Jane Eyre* (1847).

Thinking about ... biography and authorship

To begin your own process of considering how biography can be relevant to the process of reading texts, spend some time thinking about how the following extract could be useful in a reading of Dr Johnson's poetry.

> Samuel Johnson was born at Lichfield, in Staffordshire, on the 18th of September, 1709; and his initiation into the Christian Church was not delayed; for his baptism is recorded, in the register of St Mary's parish in that city, to have been performed on the day of his birth. His father is there stiled Gentleman, a circumstance of which an ignorant panegyrist has praised him for not being proud; when the truth is, that the appellation of Gentleman, though now lost in the indiscriminate assumption of Esquire, was commonly taken by those who could not boast of gentility. His father was Michael Johnson, a native of Derbyshire, of obscure extraction, who settled in Lichfield as a bookseller and stationer. His mother was Sarah Ford, descended of an ancient race of substantial yeomanry in Warwickshire. They were well advanced in years when they married, and never had more than two children, both sons; Samuel, their first born, who lived to be the illustrious character whose various excellence I am to endeavour to record, and Nathanael, who died in his twenty-fifth year.
>
> (from James Boswell, *Boswell's Life of Johnson*, part 1 (1791))

Introduction

When we first learn to read we give little thought to the author of the words we are reading. In fiction, for example, it is the imaginary world we become lost in, and the text is everything. Many younger children wouldn't even be able to tell you the name of the author of their favourite book. As we develop into teenage readers, the issue of authorship can become more important – we might develop a craving for the works of one particular author (J. K. Rowling, Terry Pratchett, etc.) or for a collection of authors who write in a specific genre. Then, increasingly, as our education progresses the importance of the role of the author becomes enshrined – we write about 'the author's intentions' as part of our school work, or consider 'the way the author imparts meaning' in our college exams.

Which means that by the time we arrive at university, armed with the skills and approaches of reading that have served us well, we tend to be fully fledged advocates of the idea that an author's life is worthy of study as part of the reading of the texts s/he has written. We might show ourselves keen to tell our tutors and fellow students about the ways in which (say) the harrowing life of Sylvia Plath can be read through her poetry, or how the narrative of *David Copperfield* can be read as Charles Dickens's autobiography. And it tends to be at this moment that the ground gets taken from beneath us; the moment when a tutor first introduces us to the idea of the 'Death' of the author. Reading texts is unlikely ever to be quite the same after that. But before we get to the ideas of Roland Barthes, it is worthwhile considering the ways in which the role of the author has been discussed by other critics.

The role of the author

The idea that authorial biography was a necessary element of the reading of texts was perhaps best (if not first) exemplified by Samuel Johnson's *Lives of the English Poets*. This used the extensive biographical study of a large number of poets (ranging from Abraham Cowley to John Milton, Rochester to Dryden, Addison to Congreve, Gay to Pope, Swift to Watts, and Edward Young to Thomas Gray) to inform its textual criticism. For Johnson, 'no species of writing seems more worthy of cultivation than biography'.[1] The short individual discussions of specific poets included brief chronologies of their lives and careers, followed by more detailed biographies, and concluding with specific analysis of their poetry. The criticism was highly personal and subjective, and largely lacking in any coherent critical method other than Johnson's own personal impressions. His introduction of the work of Thomas Gray, for example, notes that: 'Gray's poetry is now to be considered; and I hope not to be looked on as an enemy to his name; if I confess that I contemplate it with less pleasure than his life.'[2] It is thus rather ironic that *Lives of the English Poets* also contains a caution that biographical criticism should not become overly personal or familiar: 'The Life of Cowley ... has been written by Dr Spratt ... [whose] zeal of friendship, or ambition of eloquence, has produced a funeral oration rather than a history: he has given the character, not the life of Cowley.'[3]

T. S. Eliot, writing in the twentieth century, rejected such biographical interpretation on the grounds that although it shed light on the poet, 'it is not relevant to our understanding of *the poetry as poetry*'.[4] For him there was 'in all great poetry, something which must remain unaccountable however complete might be our knowledge of the poet' (p. 112). This 'something ... unaccountable' would be jeopardized if readers and critics utilized biographical material as part of their textual criticism, and in avoiding using it the integrity, the specialness, of the text was better maintained: 'When the poem has been made, something new has happened, something that cannot be wholly explained by *anything that went before*. That, I believe, is what we mean by "creation"' (p. 112). The implication was that the reader/critic had to let certain aspects of the text remain unexplained.

As a counterweight to Eliot, other critical works from the earlier twentieth century were rooted in ideas of authorship. Freud's 'Creative Writers and Day-Dreaming' (1907), for example, saw the author as having a key role within the text itself. For Freud texts were the result of authorial anxieties and psychological tensions, embodiments of oedipal crises, penis envy, desire, and psychosexual stages. This imagined all texts as (in a sense) autobiographical, with the life of the author woven into the text. Later twentieth-century psycho-analytic literary criticism (much influenced by Freud) continued in this vein, focusing on (for instance) difficult parent–child relationships within texts, depictions of sexual development and maturation, and has shown a sensitivity to the distinction between the conscious and unconscious levels of experience. In particular, psychoanalytic methods have been used to interpret texts in terms of the unconscious objectives and desires of both author and characters.

Various Marxist critical approaches were also broadly reliant on recognition that the author played a key part in the construction of textual meaning. In particular, there was the broad Marxist principle that the basis for individual behaviour was the economic or class position in society (something that could be traced back to the political and economic philosophy first articu-lated by Karl Marx and Friedrich Engels in *The Communist Manifesto* (1848)). This principle recognized, by implication, that the life of the writer, and in particular the relationships a writer (within a particular set of class circum-stances) had with the world around them, underpinned any text they might produce. The economic position of the author was seen to influence (in some cases determine) artistic choices, decisions and actions. Writers and texts were indicators of class position, implying a rejection of the notion of the text as a universal and timeless work of genius, and seeing it instead as a marker of a particular phase in social and economic history. Seeing authors as inevitably located in relation to broader social and class movements risked downplaying the uniqueness of the role of the artist as an individual, but at the same time it clearly reinforced the importance of the author in the process of creating text and meaning.

....

Thinking about … an author's background

Consider the advantages and disadvantages of reading a text in the light of the author's psychology and/or class position.

....

Theories of the author

There are thus a range of different perspectives on the role and importance of the author in our literary-critical history. But it was not until the later twentieth century that scepticism as to the extent to which the author should be considered as part of the process of creating the meaning of the text was most clearly voiced. That came with Roland Barthes' essay, 'The Death of the Author' (1968), which is one of the most influential texts that university students will come across on the subject of authorship and textual meaning. It has been *so* influential that it is worth spending some time looking at the essay in its contentiousness and complexity. And, because of its radical central argument (even now it retains an incisive critical edge), it is important to read the essay with an open mind and accept the fact that it will try to push you in directions of thought that you might not necessarily want to go in.

Roland Barthes, 'The Death of the Author' (1968)

The first thing to say is that for the new undergraduate student of textual/literary study, this essay can be difficult. Not only is it philosophically complex, it is also estranging and alienating at times in the language it uses. Its broad argument, that it is not possible to connect any piece of writing with an origin, and in particular an originator (author), might at first appear to contradict your own common sense; we might all cite examples of writing that seems very clearly to carry with it the identity or life of the author, and be loaded with intentions and meanings as a result. Think of the First World War poetry of Wilfred Owen or Siegfried Sassoon, for example, laced with the melancholy mourning of the deaths of countless young men on the battlefields of Europe. Is it really feasible to argue, we might ask, that the 'point of origin' (i.e. the author) has no place in our reading of these texts?

So, Barthes' essay encouraged readers to reject the idea that the role of the author in the production of textual meaning was significant: 'The birth of the reader must be at the cost of the death of the Author,'[5] he stated. This was in opposition to the critical orthodoxy wherein: 'The *author* still reigns in histories of literature, biographies of writers, interviews, magazines, as in the very consciousness of men of letters anxious to unite their person and their work through diaries and memoirs' (p. 114). Barthes displaced this orthodoxy with the idea that when 'writing begins … the author enters into his own death' (p. 114), which was a reaction against the way in which 'ordinary culture is tyranni-cally centred on the author, his person, his life, his tastes, his passions' (p. 114). The idea was to overcome the explanation of a text 'always sought in the man or woman who produced it, as if it were always in the end … the voice of a single person, the *author* "confiding" in us' (p. 115).

In denying the importance of the author, Barthes argued that language had a life of its own, that it 'performs' (p. 115) the creation of meaning in its own right, divorced from authorial intentions. This emphasized the role of readers and the meanings they ascribed to words and phrases and sentences. Barthes cited the example of 'automatic writing', wherein the hand of the writer wrote arbitrarily, with the head 'switched off', and surrealist projects where groups of writers worked together to produce a collaborative text, as examples of how the focus on the status and power of the author could be misleading. He pushed this conclusion to its ultimate implication – stating that texts themselves carried with them no innate meanings, and that meanings emerged only once the reader had created them: 'the whole of the enunciation is an empty process, functioning perfectly without there being any need for it to be filled with the person of the interlocutors' (p. 116). This made the reader *the* key element in the author-reader-text relationship, transforming 'the modern text … the text is henceforth made and read in such a way that at all its levels the author is absent' (p. 116).

The whole notion of the 'death' of the author reacted against the type of criticism within which it was seen as possible, desirable even, to establish the intention of the author and consequently (often) a single meaning of the text. This was decried by New Critics (discussed in Chapter 3) as the 'intentional fallacy'. The idea of 'The Death of the Author' was that in escaping such notions texts would be freed up to fresh readings: 'We know now that a text is not a line of words releasing a single "theological" meaning (the "message" of the Author-God) but a multi-dimensional space in which a variety of writings, none of them original, blend and clash. The text is a tissue of quotations drawn from the innumerable centres of culture' (p. 116). This meant that the modern reader/critic was to have a very different relationship with the text than the reader of the past: 'once the Author is removed, the claim to decipher a text becomes quite futile. [For] to give a text an Author is to impose a limit on that text, to furnish it with a final signified, to close the writing' (p. 117).

As far as Barthes was concerned, there would always be resistance to the jetti-soning of the idea of author because the idea of the author 'suits criticism very well', giving readers and critics 'the important task of discovering the Author

... beneath the work: when the Author has been found, the text is "explained" – victory to the critic' (p. 117). Which explained why, for him, 'the reign of the Author has also been that of the Critic' (p. 117). Barthes' celebration of the role of the reader was thus also his response to what he saw as the 'tyranny' of the critic: 'A text is made of multiple writings, drawn from many cultures and entering into mutual relations of dialogue, parody, contestation, but there is one place where this multiplicity is focused and that place is the reader, not, as was hitherto said, the author' (p. 118).

Barthes' essay presents a number of difficulties for undergraduate university readers, both in terms of the complexity of some of its language and also because the ideas it contains are extremely challenging. But the fact is that the essay has been enormously significant as a fundamental questioning of one of the most pervasive assumptions across the large majority of our literary-critical history – that the author is an important figure in the creation of texts and their meaning. Barthes denies that assumption, as well as the associated notion that a text is the product not just of a particular author but also of an identifiable historical period. He pushes us towards the idea that textual meaning is a collaborative process in which readers, language and the cultures of which they are a part all participate.

....

Thinking about ... overlooking the author

Make the case for NOT considering the author within a textual reading.

....

Theories of reading

A key implication of Barthes' essay was that a greater focus had to be placed on the role of the *reader* in the creation of meaning. And this was paralleled by the work of a significant number of critics/theorists who developed philosophies of reading and interpretation that privileged the role of the reader within the process by which this meaning was achieved. Two of the more high-profile theories in this area were *Reader-Response Criticism* and *Reception Theory*. The next sections of this chapter will consider such critical approaches, approaches that embodied an acceptance of the 'death' of the author. The chapter will then look at critical methods that have resisted this 'death' and found ways of keeping the author at the heart of the process of considering what texts mean.

Reader-response criticism

'Reader-response criticism' has been the term used to describe a range of theories of reading and interpretation that shared a focus on the role of the reader in the creation of textual meaning. There never was a coherent 'school' of critics who were working together on the basis of their shared interest, more a loose acceptance by all that the reader was the key figure in understanding texts. The process of reading was seen as key in bringing the text into being. There was, in this way, an implied tension between reader-centred theories and other critical approaches that saw the text as existing prior to the reader's involvement, a text being 'out there' waiting to be understood rather than interpreted. These latter approaches included close reading methods such as New Criticism and Practical Criticism.

A text, anyone?

The debate about what is meant by 'the text' is complex and wide-ranging; it touches on various theoretical approaches, such as semiotics, linguistics and cultural studies. For some past theorists, 'the text' did not exist; it only came into being when there was a reader interpreting: 'Meaning is a transitive phenomenon. It is not a *thing* that texts can *have*, but is something that can only be produced, and always differently, within the reading formations that regulate the encounters between texts and readers.'[6] For Tony Bennett, reading was reliant on an interaction 'between the *culturally activated* text and the *culturally activated* reader, an interaction structured by the material, social, ideological, and institutional relationships in which *both* text and readers are inescapably inscribed' (p. 216). Therein the cultural background of both the reader and the text were of central importance in the interpretive process, in forming and shaping the nature of any and every interpretation. This was also recognized by Stanley Fish, who argued that texts do 'not lie innocently in the world but are themselves constituted by an interpretive act, even if, as is often the case, that act is unacknowledged.'[7]

The focus of reader-response criticism

Reader-response critics focused on the relationships between readers and language, on the psychological dimensions of the reading experience and the cultural and social aspects of reading and interpretation. The emphasis varied across the work of Umberto Eco (1932–), Stanley Fish (1938–), Hans-Robert Jauss (1921–97) and Wolfgang Iser (1926–2007), among others, as did the extent to which the existence of 'the text' was denied or qualified; there was some debate about the actual nature of the reader and in particular as to whether reading was an individual or a collective process. But each of these critics, in their own way, was concerned with the response of readers to texts, which were viewed as indicative of the culture to which they belonged, or else as part of a more individual psychological or ideological process. This led to the readers' responses themselves (as much as the texts they were responding to) becoming the object of study.

The assumptions of reader-response criticism

Although there are different reader-response theories, they all share a number of common assumptions:

- That texts have no single, fixed meanings; reading is not about uncovering the 'truth' of the text.
- That to read is to collaborate in a process akin to a performance, bringing 'texts' (and there are varying views as to what this term means) to life.
- That texts do not exist until they are read, or else they are entirely reliant on a reader/readers to enact them.
- That readers' individual and collective responses are relevant to an understanding of texts as well as to an understanding of the readers themselves and the cultures to which they belong.

These assumptions have underpinned critical discussions of the reader responses of professional or published readers, critics, students and the general public. Some of these have looked at the extent to which readers interpret texts in terms of their own experience or else in terms of a wider moral, cultural or political viewpoint, and they have also at times considered hidden or disguised meanings. Reader-response criticism has looked at the ways in which readings reflect the cultural attitudes of the time in which the readers lived (which can allow for historical comparison), examined how the knowledge of the reader impacts upon their reading of texts, and attempted to unearth a common basis for reading and interpretation across particular groups of readers.

The benefits of reader-response criticism

One of the great potentials of reader-response theory, particularly in relation to the discussion of creativity and critical practice that began in Chapter 2, is that it allows for reading to be seen as a kind of creative performance in its own right. Freed from the restrictions of thinking that they must read in particular ways, readers are encouraged to encounter texts in their own way, to explore them and experience them at a range of levels (intellectual/emotional/psychological/cultural, etc.). Readers then create their own meanings, create their own texts even. Which brings us back to Roland Barthes and his notion of the different types of engagement readers have with texts:

> Our evaluation can be linked only to a practice, and this practice is that of writing. On the one hand, there is what it is possible to write, and on the other, what it is no longer possible to write: what is within the practice of the writer and what has left it: which texts would I consent to write (to re-write), to desire, to put forth as a force in this world of mine? What evaluation finds is precisely this value: what can be written (rewritten) today: the *writerly*.[8]

This quality of writerly-ness was important for Barthes, because 'the goal of literary work (of literature as work) is to make the reader no longer a consumer, but a producer of the text' (p. 4). This idea counteracted what he saw as the modern tendency towards the passive reading of texts: 'The reader is thereby plunged into a kind of idleness – he is intransitive; he is, in short, *serious*: instead of functioning himself, instead of gaining access to the magic of the signifier, to the pleasure of writing, he is left with no more than the poor freedom either to accept or reject the text: reading is nothing more than a *referendum*' (p. 4). It was the responsibility of the 'readerly' text, standing in opposition to the 'writerly' text, to allow greater and more expansive interpretations.

Reception theory

'Reception theory' emerged as a close relation to reader-response criticism, something illustrated by the fact that the most well-known reception theorist, Hans-Robert Jauss, was also seen by many as a reader-response critic. But reception theory was particular in the way that it focused on the importance of the reader's interpretation of the text. It concentrated on how readers interacted with texts based on their lived experience and individual background (social, cultural, political), and this interaction was seen as resulting in the *meaning* of the text. As such, the focus was just as much on the nature of these responses as it was on the textual readings that emerged. Thus, examining how readers from particular cultural backgrounds interpreted texts was not the end of the story; reception theorists used these interpretations to infer conclusions about the similarities and dissimilarities between cultures and historical periods by analysing the ways in which different groups of readers read.

Thinking about ... the power of the reader

What limit is there on the power of 'the reader' to create the meaning of a text?

The significance of biography

Despite the impact of the idea of the 'death' of the author, for many critics it is important that the author was not overlooked. And, once this principle is accepted, it follows that a writer's biography has a place within the process of interpreting texts. For undergraduate students this is often a comfort. The problem, however, is that there is a strong temptation to utilize biography in an overly stringent fashion, reducing textual readings to forms of literary autobiography.

And so the focus on an author's life can be both liberating and restricting at the same time – to try to establish (for example) Freudian patterns in the work of Virginia Woolf, or connect the life of Aphra Behn to an emergent tradition of female authorship, can be worthwhile and imaginative. However, if this criticism means that the works of Woolf and Behn becoming effectively imprisoned within the author's own biography, viewed as symptoms of a life, then the biographical approach inhibits the reading process rather than facilitating it.

To avoid this pitfall, the reader has to understand how biography can be utilized productively. And to do so, it helps to bear in mind Stella Tillyard's comment that: 'Biography ... often gives intimacy without context, and history without biography offers context without the warmth of individual lives.'[9] For biography allows a particular way in to texts, and can be a useful supplement to contextual readings. But it would be a mistake to overlook the fact that biography is itself part of a broader historical context. The lives of authors do not unfold within a vacuum, and it is important for readers to understand how biography fits within the broader historical frame. To focus simply on the events of a life, and to attempt to tie these in to specific moments of any text without considering the broader historical context, only delivers a fraction of the story.

The limitations of author-centred approaches

There are, however, particular challenges in adopting author-centred critical approaches. First, there is the question as to whether it is ever possible to understand an author's intentions:

- How can any contemporary critic, regardless of their access to a range of research and source materials, comprehend the mindset of an author?
- How is it possible for us to gain anything more than a vague approximation of how specific writers *might* have been feeling or thinking, based on our own interpretations?
- Surely, the best we can achieve is a vague *estimation* of what we take to be the writer's point-of-view?

For those critics who accept the universal quality of human nature, such problems are drastically reduced. For them, authors in times past would share assumptions and values with authors of the present, and so the interpretative gap between one and the other would be less apparent. Which would mean that critics could talk about the intentions of (say) Aphra Behn with a greater confidence that they could achieve empathy and understanding. For those who reject universalism, there can be no such confidence.

The second area of difficulty with author-centred criticism is that the issue of authorial intention is problematic whether or not you believe in universalism, whether or not you are studying authors of the past or authors of the present, because it relies on an idea of writerly (human) self-awareness in authors that some see as untenable. Living as we do in a world after Freud and with the by now commonplace recognition of the human subconscious, it is hard to argue that human beings are always aware of their own intentions and motivations. As such, it is difficult to argue that we as readers can definitively establish what an author's intentions were when they were writing particular texts. Because the truth is, *they might not have even been aware themselves*. The human subconscious is thus surely beyond the easy comprehension of literary critics?

The third danger with author-centred approaches is the over-reliance on biographical interpretation. Any use of biography to help develop a piece of textual criticism must be carried out with reservations. These reservations are to do with the need to evaluate your biographical material, critique the evidence and not simply to assume that all information is, in and of itself, valuable to the critic as part of a reading. Furthermore, this biographical material, however relevant it might seem, should never lead to reading literary texts *as* autobiography. Such criticism does little justice to the texts themselves, implying a simplistic creative process wherein authors simply recycle their own life experience in each text they create. Therein texts are reduced to a single denominator, the author's life-story. So the important thing to remember is that biographical detail *can* bring a textual reading to life, but it can also lead to a reader overlooking what is special or unique about a given text.

Healthy scepticism

This is why, when deploying biographical information in textual readings, we need to adopt a position of what I call *healthy scepticism*. This is where the reader/critic:

- acknowledges the important role the author has to play in creating meaning. It seems odd to have to say so, but texts are written by *people*, with all the implications this brings with it.
- evaluates their own position in terms of the loaded question of universal human nature and thinks through the implications of this in terms of how they understand texts.
- understands the implications of theoretical approaches that question the role of the author, as well as those that privilege authorial intention as key to understanding texts.
- accepts that biographical material has a role to play in reading, while developing the necessary critical skills to be able to handle such material in a way that does not reduce the text to the status of a mirror on the personal life of the author.

Creative exploration: biography and authorship

For some, biography (or life writing) is not criticism at all; to write someone's life is seen as a creative exercise, closer to creative writing than textual criticism. Yet this hasn't always been the case. When James Boswell wrote his famous biography of Samuel Johnson this was seen as a major literary-critical achievement. And when Dr Johnson himself wrote his lengthy *Lives of the English Poets* (which relied heavily on biography and biographical interpretation throughout) there was no question of this being dismissed for its lack of *critical* relevance.

So it is important to recognize that the act of writing and reading biography can spark off aspects of textual discussion that might otherwise be neglected. It is an interesting exercise, when writing about a text, to write a short biography of the author as part of your research, and then to use this biography to open up readings of the text being studied. What you quickly find is that some of the details that you judged to be important/worthy enough to be included in your biography don't necessarily help very much when it comes to developing an analysis of a text. Other biographical details, on the other hand, begin an exciting train of thought (one idea developing into another) that results in various insights into the text. It is not possible to say, at the outset, which pieces of information will become more relevant than others – but by working through your mini-biography you will soon find that out for yourself. Crucially, this process will illustrate a positive relationship between your own creative exploration of the biography of an author and your critical examination of texts written by them. Your creative work will become part of your own critical reading, helping it to achieve a more imaginative, lively, innovative feel.

Task 1: Starting with biography

- Write a 300-word biography of the author of any text you are studying. In preparing this you will be required to use research skills in appraising a range of biographical materials on a single subject; critical skills in selecting what you judge to be the most important details of the writer's life; writing skills (especially concision and accuracy) in capturing this life in a limited number of words; and creative skills in choosing how to represent your material in a way that adequately and effectively conveys what you have gleaned from your research.

Task 2: Biography into something else

- Examine your text in the light of this biography. What areas of interpretation does it open up to you, what readings does it introduce/suggest?

Task 3: Evaluating your responses

- Make a list of the ways in which the information in your biography was helpful in developing your reading of the text.
- Make a second list of the ways in which the information in your biography was *not* helpful in developing your reading of the text.

Task 4: The other side of the story

- Identify another text you know well, written by an author you know little or nothing about; think and make notes about the text (plot, characters, issues, etc.). Are there aspects of the text that would become more clear if you had additional information about the author?

Task 5: Placing things in context

- How important do you judge it to be that readers keep the author in mind when they are interpreting a text?
- To what extent do you think that the author is the person who makes the text's meaning?
- How can readers know what an author intended? Is it important to do so?
- If it isn't the author who creates textual meaning, how is it created? Consider the various alternatives.

Critical reading: Charlotte Brontë, *Jane Eyre*

Jane Eyre has a rich potential for a biographical reading. Indeed, the novels of all the Brontë sisters lend themselves to such a biographical interpretation; from Anne's *Agnes Grey* and *The Tenant of Wildfell Hall* to Charlotte's *Villette* and *The Professor* to Emily's *Wuthering Heights*. *Jane Eyre*, specifically, focuses on an only slightly disguised version of Charlotte Brontë's life at school, her time as a governess and her life as an unmarried woman in mid-nineteenth-century England.

In truth, these are aspects of the novel that have been regularly written about within Brontë criticism. This is why my initial outline biographical reading of the novel will focus on a different aspect of Brontë biography, namely the family connection with Ireland and keen interest in Anglo-Irish history and politics. For it is only over the last decade or so that critics have begun to consider a potential Irish dimension to the novel and to produce new readings that focus on it. Which means that anything that is said about this dimension of *Jane Eyre* will be relatively fresh and contribute to what is a (relatively) less cultivated dimension of the novel.

The Reverend Patrick Brontë came to England from Ireland with his family in 1820, settling in Haworth, Yorkshire. Subsequently there was an ongoing family connection with Ireland and there is evidence that the family kept in regular touch with the Irish wing of the family as well as maintaining a keen interest in Irish history and politics. Part of this interest in Ireland can be seen in the family reading habits; it was commonplace for the Brontës to sit around the kitchen table of an evening and read to each other, and a particular favourite was Irish literature, especially mythical and legendary tales.

When Charlotte Brontë was eventually published herself this was under a pseudonym (as was also true of her sisters). This was in part an attempt to prevent readers becoming aware of the fact that she was a woman. To write fiction as a woman was at this time (the early Victorian period) still frowned upon by many critics and readers, and so many women wrote as men or under non-gendered names to prevent the critics/readers judging them negatively before they had even begun reading what they had written. So from the very beginning of her writing career Charlotte Brontë was aware of a need for disguise in writing and publishing.

Another biographical detail to consider is the way in which Charlotte reworked her earlier literary writings later in her career. Three stories that she wrote as a younger woman, 'Albion and Marina', 'An Adventure in Ireland' and 'Zamorna and Mina Laury' were reused in her later, more mature texts. Interestingly, although these stories each had Irish elements originally, in rewriting them Brontë lost much of the Irish dimension, something perhaps not surprising bearing in mind the controversy of Ireland in the 1840s after the Great Famine. At this time Ireland became a troubling subject matter for many English readers and so writers tended to steer clear of the subject alltogether. One who did not, Anthony Trollope, paid for his decision to write two Irish novels (*The Macdermots of Ballycloran* (1847) and *The Kellys and the O'Kellys* (1848)) at the beginning of his career with their spectacular commercial failure.

Each of these snippets of biographical information should encourage readers to look again at the narrative of *Jane Eyre*, thinking about how the Irish background of the Brontë family might have had an impact on the development of the novel. In what ways might it, for example, have a 'hidden' or disguised Irish subject matter?

And it is not long before ideas begin to emerge. For example, it is clear that the theme of marriage is very prominent in *Jane Eyre*. There is a marriage of deceit in the case of Rochester and Bertha Mason, the attempted fraudulent marriage of Rochester and Jane and the proposal of an unequal marriage by St John Rivers to Jane. It is only at the end of the novel that there is the 'perfect concord' of the marriage of equals, achieved by Jane and Rochester. True, it is achieved by rather contrived means – Rochester has to be emasculated by losing part of his sight and not being able to walk (thereby requiring Jane as nurse), but nevertheless the harmony of the ending strikes a contrast with the visions of marriage that have preceded it.

All of this means that, to a large extent, the narrative functions as a demonstration of the types of marital union that will not work, and eventually the type of marriage that should be aspired to. Which has a particular relevance when we realize that during the nineteenth century the idea of there being a 'marriage' between England and Ireland was commonplace, with critics and commentators arguing that (either) this should be a marriage of equals with Ireland as a true partner or else that England should be the dominant, usually masculine partner and Ireland the submissive (feminine) one. This political debate about 'marriage' can thus be related to the depiction of marriage in the novel, reading Jane as a disguised version of Ireland and Rochester a symbolic form of England.

Making this leap of interpretation then pushes the reader back into the text to reconsider key moments of the plot:

> 'you are a dependant, Mama says; you have no money ... you ought to beg, and not live here with gentleman's children like us, and eat the same meals we do', or 'you ought not to think yourself on an equal-ity with the Misses Reed and Master Reed, because Missis Reed kindly allows you to be brought up with them. They will have a great deal of money, and you will have none: it is your place to be humble, and to try to make yourself agreeable to them.' (Chapter 1)

Just such an accusation of stifling dependency was levelled at Irish people throughout the years of famine and economic hardship, the precise years during which *Jane Eyre* was written. The Catholic Irish in particular were seen by many English as poor relations, demanding charity and showing no gratitude for anything they received.

So at once this biographical information about the Brontës and Ireland pushes the reader into reconsidering Jane's struggle for equality in the novel. For what she seeks, ultimately through marriage, is a social position based on mutual esteem and greater equality. Such an idea of marriage as is achieved by Jane and Rochester is exactly that which was advocated by those sympathetic to the Irish cause as the only just solution to the problems of Anglo-Irish relations during the mid-nineteenth century. *Jane Eyre* can be seen in this light as providing a disguised parallel between the life of its heroine and the status of Ireland (in relation to England) during the mid-nineteenth century. Brontë, it could be claimed, who understood the key political issues through her family connec-tions, and who was also personally aware of the need for disguise when writing fiction when presenting issues that could alienate the readership (such as her own gender as an author), thus developed a range of textual parallels between the plot of *Jane Eyre* and contemporaneous Anglo-Irish relations that were rather more than mere coincidences.[10]

Whether or not you accept this outline reading of *Jane Eyre*, rooted as it is in the biography of the author, the wider point is that biographical detail has enormous potential to bring texts to life. It can highlight particular aspects of texts and help readers make connections they did not previously notice. At the same time, readers must bear in mind the risks of critical readings that are over-reliant on such a biographical dimension, wherein the text has little else to say other than that which concerns the life of the author. Novels, poems and plays are *not* autobiographies. But that is not to say that they do not include autobiographical detail, or that they are not based (at times) on biographical events. It is the job of the reader/critic to decide where to draw the line between life and text.

Checkpoint 3

This chapter has given context to discussions about the role of the author in creating the text and illustrated different ways in which considering the author can affect how readers interpret their work. The chapter has also considered different ways in which biographical information about the author can be useful in reading. In order to assess your knowledge and understanding of these issues, attempt the following series of questions designed to test what you have learnt. These can be for individual reflection or be used as the basis for seminar discussion.

- In what ways have you used biographical information about authors before? Was it successful?
- When do you think having biographical knowledge could prove to be a disadvantage rather than an advantage?
- Are there some authors/texts that might be more sensitive to a biographical reading than others?

Suggested further reading

Ackroyd, P., *Dickens* (1990) – a detailed example of critical biography.
—— *Shakespeare: the Biography* (2005) – more of the same.
Barthes, R., 'The Death of the Author' (1968) – hugely influential on subsequent critical approaches.
—— *S/Z* (1970) – important for its recognition of the difference between 'readerly' and 'writerly' texts (in terms of the ways in which they interact with their audiences).
Boswell, J., *Boswell's Life of Johnson* (1791) – a classic earlier literary biography.
Fish, S., *Is there a Text in this Class?* (1980) – important in understanding the complexities of reader–text relationships.
Gaskell, E., *Life of Charlotte Brontë* (1857) – another influential literary biography.
Johnson, S., *Lives of the English Poets* (1781) – volumes in which the boundaries between biography and textual criticism blur.

Stepping things up

Once you have completed all the exercises in this chapter and feel comfortable that you have absorbed the ideas, perspectives and approaches it has discussed, you are ready to engage in some more challenging work:

(1) What hints about the life of Arthur Conan Doyle are suggested by 'The Man with the Twisted Lip' (which can be found in Appendix C)?

(2) Consider how readers of the past might have interpreted 'The Man with the Twisted Lip' differently from contemporary readers.

(3) To what extent is 'The Man with the Twisted Lip' a 'writerly' text, allowing the reader opportunities to interpret the narrative in a variety of ways?

History and contexts

5

Chapter summary

This chapter will begin by looking at how the contexts of a text can be taken into account within the process of reading and critical interpretation. The strengths as well as the limitations of these contextual approaches will also be examined. Specific critical approaches that have privileged contextual reading will be discussed, ranging from Plato to structuralism, new historicism, Marxism, feminism and post-colonial criticism. Ultimately, a historical-contextual approach will be 'road tested' through a reading of Toni Morrison's novel *Beloved* (1987).

Thinking about ... history and contexts

To begin your own process of considering how the reading of texts can take account of history and other contexts, spend some time thinking about how your reading of the following extract might be enhanced by additional historical information.

> He [Tom] dressed, put on one of his new nonwrinkling travelling suits, and strolled out into the Palermo dusk. There across the plaza was the great Norman-influenced cathedral he had read about, built by the English archbishop Walter-of-the-Mill, he remembered from a guide-book. Then there was Siracusa to the south, scene of a mighty naval battle between the Latins and the Greeks. And Dionysus' Ear. And Taormina. And Etna! It was a big island and brand-new to him. Sicilia! Stronghold of Giuliano! Colonized by the ancient Greeks, invaded by Norman and Saracen! Tomorrow he would commence his tourism properly, but this moment was glorious, he thought as he stopped to stare at the tall, towered cathedral in front of him. Wonderful to look at the dusty arches of its façade and to think of going inside tomorrow, to imagine its musty, sweetish smell, composed of the uncounted candles and incense-burnings of hundreds and hundreds of years.
>
> (from Patricia Highsmith, *The Talented Mr Ripley*, Chapter 19 (1955))

Reading contexts

The idea that context(s) have a key role in the production and understanding of texts can be traced back as far as classical Greek literary criticism, which was explicitly and particularly concerned with the relationship between texts and the political and moral context of their times. Politics and morality were viewed by a number of the early, seminal critics (including Plato and Aristotle) as inescapable concerns for writers of all kinds. Thus, it is perhaps no surprise to find that this concern with history and contexts is still such a concern of many contemporary critics, to a point where these days it would be difficult to imagine that critical studies of texts that completely *ignored* all forms of context would be accepted for publication by publishers or journals.

Types of context

Different critics have tended to utilize contexts in different ways within their reading of texts. However, there are broad strands of contextual criticism:

- Genre
- Literary history
- Authorial biography (discussed at length in Chapter 4)
- History

Each of these seeks to specifically relate texts to an element of their background, as a way of enlightening them; in understanding the frame within which a particular text sits, the work itself is illuminated in new ways. To understand how these different contexts can inform the reading process in different ways, it is first necessary to examine the types of context that can be utilized.

Genre

The focus on how texts relate to ideas of *genre* (a distinctive style, form or content) is perhaps best understood as part of the development of structuralist criticism in the twentieth century. For this placed texts in relation to the various 'structures' of literary history, namely the genres that could shed light on how texts worked and how they related to certain conventions of form and style. In Northrop Frye's *Anatomy of Criticism* (1957), for example, Frye's narratological approach was concerned with the structures and functions of narrative form and the ways in which narratives worked to achieve specific effects. Narratology tended to look not just at the individual text, but at that text within the context of other texts (e.g. a story within the context of stories), and to consider the nature of this relationship. So, in a critical work such as Vladimir Propp's *The Morphology of the Folktale* (1958), Propp examined the relationship between stories and plots (also known as *fabula* vs. *sjuzhet*), looking for patterns and recurring structures in the way stories have been told. He was not so much interested in the *content* of these stories. As such, this type of critical reading worked towards seeing the common elements of narratives rather than the differences between them.

Although the consideration of the genre conventions of texts is a refinement of a broadly structuralist critical method, a general critical concern with these conventions can be traced back to before the emergence of structuralism. Percy Bysshe Shelley, for example, wrote of the necessary interaction between writers and textual forms in the early nineteenth century:

> It is impossible that anyone who inhabits the same age with such writers as those who stand in the foremost ranks of our own, can conscientiously assure himself that his language and tone of thought may not have been modified by the study of the productions of those extraordinary intellects. It is true, that, not the spirit of their genius, but *the forms in which it has manifested itself*, are due less to the peculiarities of their own minds than to the peculiarity of the moral and intellectual condition of the minds among which they have been produced. [my italics][1]

For Shelley, by considering the formal context of a text the critic was able to achieve a clearer understanding of the way in which writers worked and the process through which their writing took shape.

Yet there has always been a potential difficulty with contextualizing a text in terms of its genre. Such readings tend not to allow much scope for *history*; by 'history' I mean not just historical context (including social, cultural, political, economic aspects) but also the implications and effects of historical *change*. Genre contextualization is at times a little static, not recognizing or allowing for the ways in which formal conventions alter over time. Genre tends to be viewed as fixed, and discussions of genre conventions, formal properties, narrative structures, etc. look for continuities across historical periods rather than historical differences. As a result critical attention is not always paid to how genre conventions shift, with too much focus placed on the unchanging elements of genre and narrative structure. Evidence of this can be found in the work of critics who seek to identify a schema by which *all* narratives can be contained and defined, a critical approach that risks overlooking many of the variations and refinements of individual texts within a broad framework. This tendency is apparent even in a modern critical work such as Christopher Booker's *The Seven Basic Plots* (2004).

Thinking about … texts as structures

To what extent do you think it is appropriate/helpful to read texts as self-contained 'structures'?

Literary history

Readings of texts that focus upon the more general context of literary history are possibly less likely to overlook the significance of historical change. For although the discussion of how a text relates to literary history/culture can often include a consideration of genre, there are crucial differences between the two approaches. There are aspects of literary history that are not specifically related to genre and yet can provide interesting areas of discussion and debate. For a knowledge of literary history can allow the reader/critic to talk about things such as:

- whether a text was part of a wider artistic movement
- whether the form in which the text was written/published had an impact on its content
- whether a text was groundbreaking/original, and if so how

For example, discussing how a text relates to literary history provides the reader with a number of other texts (not just *forms* of text) by way of comparison and contrast. They might discuss the poetry of Thomas Hood (1799–1845), for example, in relation to the English ballad tradition, and use the tradition as a means of examining the particular concerns of Hood's writing as well as showing how his work differed from other poetry of his period. Or the reader might consider the origins of Mary Shelley's *Frankenstein* (1817) in relation to the development of the tradition of Gothic writing, and examine how Shelley's novel contributed towards the nineteenth-century understanding of the supernatural (offering comparison with the work of Horace Walpole and Ann Radcliffe, among others). Such a discussion would combine a knowledge of literary history with an ability to read specific texts in detail.

For T. S. Eliot, the consideration of the broad frame of literary history was fundamental. His notion of *tradition* relied on what he called the 'historical sense', which was indispensable to the mature poet. It allowed 'a man to write not merely with his own generation in his bones, but with a feeling that the whole of the literature of Europe from Homer and within it the whole of the literature of his own country has a simultaneous existence and composes a simultaneous order'.[2] For Eliot: 'no poet, no artist of any art, has his complete meaning alone. His significance, his appreciation is the appreciation of his relation to the dead poets and artists' (p. 25). The poet was to 'develop or procure the consciousness of the past and ... he should continue to develop this consciousness throughout his career' (p. 28).

What Eliot was anticipating here, with the astuteness of a critic and artist who was ahead of his time, was what modern critics call *intertextuality*. This is the term used to describe when a text makes allusion or reference to another text, or possibly a number of other texts. A well-known example of such an intertextual relationship was that between Jean Rhys's novel *Wide Sargasso Sea* (1966) and Charlotte Brontë's *Jane Eyre*. Rhys wrote *Wide Sargasso Sea* as a feminist response to Brontë's novel and in particular to redress the way in which *Jane Eyre* represents the life and character of Bertha Mason, Rochester's first wife. So Rhys's text brings Bertha to life and depicts the relationship she had with Rochester when they first met in the Caribbean. Rhys focuses specifically on Bertha's sexuality, the way she is treated because of her racial background, and on the harshness and lack of care Rochester shows towards her. The novel thus works as a revision of *Jane Eyre*, with its subject drawn from the many silences of Brontë's original in terms of the past history of the woman Rochester keeps imprisoned in the attic of Thornfield Hall.

Therein *Wide Sargasso Sea* and *Jane Eyre* stand in *intertextual* relation to each other. The reader of Rhys's novel can return to *Jane Eyre* with a heightened awareness of the way in which Brontë's text marginalizes Bertha, and is thus encouraged to ask questions of the original text and even to speculate as to other 'additional' readings of Brontë's narrative. The intertextual relationship is two-way, with the later text informed by the former, allowing for the reading of the earlier text to be reshaped or redirected by the existence of the latter.

••

Thinking about ... intertextuality

Identify other 'intertextual' relationships between different texts, and consider how this intertextuality works in each case.

••

Reading genre and literary history: drawbacks

The potential weakness of reading texts in relation to their genre or literary history is that (as was seen to be the case with biography) such readings can be limiting. If we read texts simply in relation to certain formal conventions or literary influences we can overlook their particularity. Thus, to examine *Frankenstein* solely in terms of the Gothic tradition could be to diminish the specific intricacies of its language, or to consider the relationship between the novel and the Romantic movement of the early nineteenth century could be to ignore the connection between the narrative and nineteenth-century ideas about science and scientific discovery. Continually referring to literary genre/history defines texts only in terms of other texts and forms, and doesn't always allow for an appreciation of the originality and particularity of a work.

History: cultural/social/political

The main advantage of using history as part of the discussion of a text is that it allows the reader/critic to introduce information and knowledge from a seemingly limitless frame of reference. This increases the possibilities of textual reading infinitely. If we assume (for purposes of argument) that we are working on a text written in 1712, then considering 'history' as part of the textual reading allows the critic to examine (as just a very few examples):

- the political background
- social formations and cultural habits
- military conflicts
- the philosophical background
- other art/writing of the period
- moral and spiritual practices and beliefs

And within each of these different categories there are numerous subdivisions to do with geography, gender, social class, ethnicity, etc., which makes the discussion of historical context a rich and fruitful method of exploration. The only problem is that the subject field is *so* potentially vast that it is a little difficult to establish where it might end. For example, to talk of social formations and cultural habits could include the ways in which people lived (towns, cities, suburbs, etc.), the role and type of education during a period, popular cultural events (fairs, carnivals, etc.), and looking at the philosophical backdrop of an era might allow consideration of a range of ideas and ideologies, political policies and agendas, legislation and religious practices, etc. To a certain extent, it is difficult to think of any aspect of culture and society that would *not* be relevant to such a textual reading.

The significance of history

The interpretation of texts through their historical context was prevalent as far back as Plato, who concerned himself with the social and political context of literature. For him, because children were unable to 'distinguish between what is allegory and what isn't, and opinions formed at that age are usually difficult to eradicate or change', it was vital that 'the first stories they hear shall aim at encouraging the highest excellence of character'.[3] Plato believed that, as a consequence, the stories had to embody the 'correct' principles and values of their era: 'The founders of a state, though they must know the type of story the poet must produce, and reject any that do not conform to that type, need not write them themselves' (p. 133). Specifically, for example, the gods could not be shown as anything other than perfect and infallible, because this might have a negative impact on society and the way in which Greek history evolved: 'we must ask the poets to stop giving their present gloomy account of the after-life, which is both untrue and unsuitable to produce a fighting-spirit, and make them speak more favourably of it' (p. 140).

So for Plato texts should not be separated from their political context or read in isolation from this. This was why he feared the influence of the writer:

> he deals with a low element in the mind ... we are therefore quite right to refuse to admit him to a properly run state, because he wakens and encourages and strengthens the lower elements in the mind to the detriment of reason, which is like giving power and political control to the worst elements in a state and ruining the better elements. (p. 435)

In order for the ideal national history to be maintained there had to be (he believed) censorship and control over the various forms of literary expression, or else 'images far removed from the truth' (p. 435) would 'corrupt even the best characters, with very few exceptions' (p. 436). The poet was a potential subversive for the way his work 'gratifies and indulges the instinctive desires of a part of us, which we forcibly restrain in our private misfortunes, with its hunger for tears and for an uninhibited indulgence in grief' (p. 436).

Such a sense of the cultural and historical importance of the poet was also apparent in the later critical writings of Shelley. Shelley saw poets as having a key role in society, taking their place as 'the unacknowledged legislators of the world'.[4] Poetry was the means by which men came to a better understanding of each other, for in deploying their own creative imaginations in reading poetry they gained insight and moral awareness, awakening love and sympathy through their active imaginations: 'to be a poet is to apprehend the true and the beautiful – in a word, the good which exists in the relations subsisting, first between existence and perception and secondly between perception and expression' (p. 279). This moral element was seen as key, for the chaos of the world could be alleviated by the highest poetry. This meant that poets were:

> the institutors of laws and the founders of civil society and the inventors of the arts of life and the teachers, who draw into a certain propinquity with the beautiful and the true that partial apprehension of the agencies of the invisible world which is called religion. (p. 279)

At the heart of this idea was a recognition that poetry was inextricably linked to its historical context, with the artistry of the words complemented by the wisdom of the political sentiments expressed.

How to Read Texts

For Matthew Arnold, just as with Shelley, the social function of texts was to improve society and culture, providing an 'inward spiritual activity', leading to 'increased sweetness, increased light, increased life, increased sympathy'.[5] Those who were engaged in creating texts were involved in 'the pursuit of perfection … the pursuit of sweetness and light'. This ensured that, when considering poetry (and, by implication, other literary forms), the critic was to keep in mind the fact that art was never to be divorced from its historical context, and consider the ways in which each text enhanced this context:

> he who works for sweetness and light, works to make reason and the will of God prevail. He who works for machinery, he who works for hatred, works only for confusion. Culture looks beyond machinery, culture hates hatred; culture has one great passion, the passion for sweetness and light. It has one even yet greater! – the passion for making them *prevail*. (p. 225)

Using history

Initially, the idea of using history to help read a text seems straightforward. The reader identifies the era from which the text emerged, researches into that historical background, then tries to find ways of establishing links between that researched background and the form and content of the text itself. For example, we can begin with the fact that Jane Austen's novel *Pride and Prejudice* appeared in 1813. And, because we know that the Napoleonic Wars (between England and France) ran from the late eighteenth century until 1815 (a history that is easy enough to research), we might then (quite reasonably) assume that there could be some form of connection between these events and Austen's novel. This conflict was likely to have been part of the early nineteenth-century mindset (we might judge), and so as a consequence any texts of that period should reflect or embody this in some way. Readers might be particularly sensitive to issues of conflict, national tension and social anxiety within Austen's narrative, in addition to looking for more direct references to particular battles or specific historical figures featuring within the Napoleonic Wars as a whole.

And yet, the more we look at the narrative of *Pride and Prejudice*, and consider exactly *how* such a military history could be used in reading the novel, the more it becomes clear that things are not as simple as first appeared. Historical readings need to be much more sophisticated than a simple tracing of events and characters onto a text. Furthermore, there are a variety of issues and questions that make the discussion of the relation between text and history highly problematic. It is these to which we turn now.

(1) The instability of history
The twentieth century was characterized by an increasing and deep-rooted

questioning of the nature of history and our ability to truly 'know' the past. And although historians and critics were asking some of the same sort of questions in earlier periods of history, in more recent times these have been asked with every-greater urgency. These questions include:

- To what extent can we rely on historical sources to give an accurate representation of the historical past?
- Because our own perspective is historical (we live within history ourselves) is our own knowledge always temporary, provisional and unreliable?
- How far can literary texts be historical?

Taken together, the clear implication of these questions is that the nature of history is in doubt, in question, up for grabs. And if we cannot satisfactorily identify a knowable 'history' to talk about confidently as we read our various texts, how can such a critical approach operate successfully?

(2) Unavailable information on some texts

Even the most optimistic of historians acknowledges that their sources are only ever partial. So there must be an inevitable recognition that there may be some information 'out there' that we do not have access to, yet which might shed a particularly helpful light on texts under consideration. This means that our textual readings can only ever be provisional at best.

(3) The issue of who knows what

The extent to which modern readers can make sound judgements as to what information is relevant to a discussion of a text written in the past is debatable. In particular, the extent to which a specific author (and a specific text) can be seen as 'knowing' about the history of their time is also in question. For example, it may be possible for a reader to identify a piece of government legislation that was contemporaneous with the text in question, such as the 1858 Divorce and Matrimonial Causes Act in the United Kingdom and Wilkie Collins's novel *The Woman in White* (published in 1860). However, demonstrating a specific and persuasive connection might be more difficult. It is possible in some cases to use the writings of the author (notes, diaries, published work, etc.) to show that they were conscious of their historical context (such as a piece of legislation), but there will always be a doubt as to the nature of the relationship between a text and this history. The reader/critic can often do no more than speculate.

NB. In the particular case cited above things might appear fairly straight-forward; Wilkie Collins was indeed aware of the Divorce Act and the wider political debate about women's rights in marriage. This might encourage us to believe that the relationship between *The Woman in White* and this history is clear. However, even when we come across what seems to be a clear textual/contextual relationship like this, there is still a significant question as to the *precise* nature of the connection and the extent to which this can be established. Ultimately, it comes down to a matter of readerly/critical interpretation.

(4) Differences between dates of composition and dates of publication
Another difficulty in using history to read texts is that there is at times a disparity between the date of publication and the date a text was created. For the careless reader, this can lead to confusion: if a textual reading begins by trying to draw a correlation between the date of publication and the political context only to find out (too late!) that the text was actually written 20 years previously and kept in a drawer, the reading collapses. An example of how this misunderstanding *could* happen is E. M. Forster's novel *Maurice*, published in 1971. The homosexual subject matter of the story seems particularly apposite as the novel was published just after Forster's death, and his homosexuality had never been revealed during his lifetime. As a result it is fairly straightforward, and (I must admit) fairly persuasive, to develop a reading of the text in terms of Forster's own deathbed 'coming out', and marking *Maurice* as a monument to the lifelong repression of his own sexuality. *However*, in fact the novel was written from about 1913, and only ever shown to Forster's close friends. Which means the reading of the text in terms of Forster acknowledging his sexuality to the world turns out to be a misreading. Sure, the novel is still a gentle homosexual romance, but it has lost *some* of its political impact in terms of being the writer's own last words on the subject of his sexuality, and instead has to be seen as further evidence of the repression that characterized his life.

(5) The question of a shared, 'collective' understanding and the notion of the unconscious
Trying to 'prove' that an author was aware of elements of his/her historical context is only ever part of the story. There are other ways in which authors and texts can imply a knowledge of their contexts, even if it is not possible beyond doubt to establish a more direct connection.

- First, there is the idea of the 'episteme': meaning a period wherein certain ideas, assumptions and philosophies were current. The word is drawn from the Greek word for 'knowledge', but its development can be traced through the work of thinkers such as the Scottish philosopher James Frederic Ferrier (1808–64) and more recently the French philosopher-critic Michel Foucault (1926–84), especially in his *Archaeology of Knowledge* (1972). The broad idea behind the 'episteme' is that particular historical periods are identified in relation to specific theories of understanding; anyone living within that period can thus absorb this 'wisdom' of ideas from the culture in which they live without necessarily studying them or even being aware of them in some cases.
- Secondly, and this is to an extent related to the notion of the 'episteme',

there is the notion of 'ideology': a coherent set of ideas or assumptions. The term is often closely linked with the development of Marxist philosophy (though in truth its origins were as much as a century before this). The term was used by early Marxists to explain why people behaved in ways that seemed to contradict their own class interests. In this sense 'ideology' referred to 'false consciousness', a veil in front of the truth preventing the working classes from rising up against their oppressors, tricking them into believing they were happy with what they had and that the world around them was fair.

More recently, the term 'ideology' has moved away from such a negative definition, towards the idea of a broader philosophy or set of beliefs underpinning social behaviour. This is the sense of the term being used in *How to Read Texts*. One of the chief characteristics of all ideologies (in this sense) is that the person who adheres to the ideology isn't necessarily aware of it; this doesn't mean that they are living in ignorance, just that they don't *recognize* their own ideology *as an ideology*. It appears to be the natural way of things. This is what the sociologist Pierre Bourdieu (1930–2002) called 'doxa'; the assumptions on which people base their lives but of which they are almost entirely unaware.

- Thirdly, there is the idea (drawn from the work of the psychoanalyst Carl Jung) of the 'collective unconscious': the notion that individual human beings possess certain ideas and exhibit certain behaviours because of their connection to a subconscious 'reservoir' of general human experiences that impact upon and influence them. This is seen to be a key element of the human condition.

The use of history within textual reading is thus made extremely problematic by this range of questions and queries about how we can establish what exactly it is and then how we can apply it successfully within our interpretation of texts. However, that has not stopped a range of critics using history as part of their reading of texts:

Marxism

At the centre of Marxist thinking was the idea that history was a narrative of struggle based on economic position, or social class. Different social classes would be dominant at different times, dependent on whether or not they held the economic power at a particular moment in history. Thus, in the nineteenth century in Britain, the middle classes were in the ascendancy because it was they who (largely) owned the factories and were the businessmen and entrepreneurs. Ultimately, Marx (1818–83) and Engels (1820–95) believed the result of years of historical class struggle would be an evening-out of economic difference, resulting is a classless society (which was itself a triumph of working-class values).

Marxist thinking, which had no explicit literary-critical dimension originally, has nevertheless been highly influential on literary criticism. In the latter half of the twentieth century in particular, Marxist-influenced critics such as Walter Benjamin (1892–1940), Georg Lukács (1885–1971), Fredric Jameson (1934–), Theodor Adorno (1903–69) and Louis Althusser (1918–90) became very popular and their works sparked a critical reconsideration of texts and contexts. Broadly, the different varieties of Marxist literary criticism focused on how texts related to the idea of class struggle, and how their form and content could be read in terms of the various stages of history that were identified within Marxist philosophy, moving towards, ultimately, a society in which the working class was dominant. Within this historical-philosophical framework, not only did the social class of the author become a key aspect of the discussion (as was revealed in Chapter 4), but the representation of characters, plots, issues and the formal properties of the text were analysed in relation to the economic circumstances within which the text emerged and also the economic and social circumstances depicted within the text itself. The impact of such analysis was to assume, almost without question, that all texts were political in nature and for readers and critics to interpret them on the basis of this.

New Historicism

New Historicism, or 'The New Historicism', was much influenced by earlier Marxist textual criticism, even though for some this relationship has been contentious. New Historicism emerged in the 1980s and became popular in the 1990s. It is still one of the most utilized critical approaches within English Studies in the UK and US. New Historicism argued that a literary text should not be studied in isolation, or viewed as the product of the individual genius of the artist. Instead, it should be placed specifically within its own historical context and viewed as a particular product of its era, location and circumstances. Further, literary and non-literary texts should be discussed in parallel in terms of the extent to which each threw light on the other. The literary text was not privileged; both literary and non-literary were given equal emphasis. The past was read as a text and there were no claims made about the possibility of accurately recovering the past in itself, only about identifying the relationships between texts within history. This marked a key difference with earlier forms of historical criticism, in which *history* was used as the informing context for the *literary* text; in New Historicism there has been no such hierarchy.

There was much in the New Historicist approach that was a response to formal/textual critical approaches such as close reading, practical criticism and New Criticism. For the New Historicists, of whom Stephen Greenblatt (1943–) has been the most well-known proponent, it was important for critics to analyse historical contexts in detail. This had two interlinked purposes: it enlivened and enriched the readings that critics produced of texts, and also (and equally importantly) readings of texts could then be used to piece together the historical/philosophical/ideological framework of specific historical eras, or epistemes. Consequently, more was learnt about the cultural and intellectual history of a period through the cumulative, incremental study of a variety of texts. The tendency of New Historicism was away from sweeping generalizations about the historical past and towards using texts as historical documents that each told a small part of the overall 'story'.

One key aspect of the New Historicist approach was the study of intertextuality, which we saw earlier in this chapter. However, within New Historicism, this intertextuality was not confined to the relationship between *literary* texts. Critics attempted to study a range of texts that were available to readers at a particular time, and tried to establish a sense of the cultural knowledge of the period. New Historicist criticism looked at the ideological influences that produced a particular text, only some of which an author might have been unaware of, which problematized the question of authorial intent. And because texts were seen as a product of ideology, New Historicism was especially interested in signs of tension and struggle within texts that were then interpreted as microcosms of wider social and political forces.

New Historicists viewed their interpretation of how texts and cultures interacted, particularly in their relationship to political power and ideology, as more subtle than that evident in earlier Marxist criticism. Michel Foucault's work was a key influence, especially texts such as *The Order of Things* (1970), *Discipline and Punish* (1975) and *The History of Sexuality* (1976). Foucault argued that the idea of literary value was flawed, as the worth or value of a text was entirely relative to its historical context – cultures decided value, there was no universal standard. The question of how texts were received within their own eras, and how readers responded to them, was a central issue.

Cultural Materialism emerged as the British parallel to the largely US-based New Historicism, looking for evidence of the ways in which texts resisted their contexts (values, assumptions, ideologies). This focus on resistance embodied a more optimistic viewpoint than that typical of New Historicism, which tended to see all resistance as ultimately contained by the text. For Cultural Materialists the past was used to read the present, so (for example) they might look at how a culture identified certain things to study or venerate, and consider what this said about its dominant value system. This explains why much Cultural Materialist criticism focused on the cultural phenomenon of Shakespeare and considered what this obsession said about the ways contemporary culture defined national identity, morality and the nature of literature. Because of its concentration on such orthodox subject matters, Cultural Materialism has been seen by some as more conservative than New Historicism, which was itself dedicated to analysing non-canonical as well as canonical works.

Thinking about ... texts and history

'It is possible for a text to avoid the influence of its historical circumstances.' Make the case both for and against this proposition.

Feminist criticism

Feminist and gender criticism grew out of the broader feminist political movement and its associated philosophies. Much of this criticism drew attention to the many assumptions/presumptions within texts that were politically loaded, especially where these assumptions overlooked or disadvantaged women. There was a feminist rediscovery of texts previously written by women but consequently largely ignored or out of print, a feminist re-reading of texts of all kinds in light of women's experiences, and an examination of how women have been represented (by both men and women) across different cultures and periods.

The two major strands of feminist critical practice were French (often called post-structuralist) feminism and Anglo-American feminism. The former tended to consider how language functioned in the construction of different gender identities, applying concepts such as 'difference' (drawn from the work of Jacques Derrida (1930–2004)), and showed the influence of Lacanian (Jacques Lacan, 1901–81) psychoanalysis in its understanding of the relationship between language and individual development. This form of feminist criticism was less explicitly concerned with the historical/social context of texts (although it was influenced by later twentieth-century feminist politics) and has been accused by some critics of being rather ahistorical in the way that it implied an unchanging female 'essence' that existed across time, almost regardless of historical circumstances.

Whether or not this criticism of French feminism is fair, it is certainly the case that what became known as Anglo-American feminism, developing out of work such as Mary Ellman's *Thinking About Women* (1968) and Kate Millett's *Sexual Politics* (1969), tended to be rather more explicit in its concern with the relationship between texts and their specific historical contexts. The analysis of texts written by women in light of female social and historical experience (what the US critic Elaine Showalter called, in her *Toward a Feminist Poetics* (1979), 'gynocritics'), or the re-evaluation of texts written by men in terms of the representation and treatment of women within those texts (what Showalter labelled 'feminist critique'), became two of the most common areas of interest in Anglo-American feminist critical readings. Crucially, both of these approaches showed themselves to be reliant on a particular view of the way in which texts interacted with their political and historical contexts, seeing them as embodiments of an ongoing, fiercely contested political-social struggle, with history a means by which it was possible to uncover and critique women's lived experiences. History was as such seen as inherently political, with texts read as key aspects of this political history.

Thinking about ... feminism and history

How can a 'feminist reading' of a text avoid history?

Post-colonial criticism

Post-colonial approaches to reading have attempted to understand how texts related to the politics and circumstances of colonialism and colonial domination, looking at (for example) signs of the aftermath of colonialism in work that emerges from newly independent nations, or else looking at the impact on cultures and societies of ongoing imperial rule. Post-colonial critics often examined texts not just to uncover the rituals, cultures and behaviours of colonized nations, but also to uncover signs of either celebration or mourning about a past or resurgent cultural identity that had been stolen or reclaimed.

Edward Said was one of the most influential thinkers in this critical-philosophical area, with his books *Orientalism* (1978) and *Culture and Imperialism* (1993) groundbreaking. They both analysed the different forms of opposition that have existed between East and West (Orient and Occident) over time and examined how these have shown themselves in a range of binary oppositions such as domestic vs. foreign, centre vs. periphery, and civilized vs. uncivilized. Other, equally influential post-colonial writings, such as Frantz Fanon's *The Wretched of the Earth* (1961), considered the impact of colonialism on the psychology of the colonized, native communities and individuals.

Part of the post-colonial critique more generally looked at national and ethnic identity and considered how these shifted according to political and social contexts. This called into question the idea of universal truth and highlighted differences of a cultural, ethnic, regional and racial kind. At the heart of this examination of the colonial experience was the idea that individuals, cultures and nations had multiple strands to their identity which interacted in different ways and at different times, and in the light of this idea texts were examined for the variety of voices and viewpoints they featured, within the context of a politically loaded interpretation of national histories.

Thinking about ... post-colonial criticism and history

To what extent must 'post-colonial' readings take into account the specific historical circumstances in which a text was produced?

The weaknesses of historical readings

(1) There is a tendency in historical readings of texts to stretch the text to fit the history that is being considered. Readers/critics sometimes seem compelled to make their versions of history 'work' for them, almost regardless of the effectiveness of the reading and what the text actually says. Think, for example, of the biographical-historical reading of Charlotte Brontë's *Jane Eyre* I offered in Chapter 4. A range of information about the 'history' of the novel and its development was referred to and pulled together into a skeleton reading of the text in terms of Irish history and politics during the mid-nineteenth century. Now, some readers will have judged this interpretation to be forced; they will have doubted whether there was sufficient evidence within the text itself to support such a reading and felt that the text was being manipulated to make it fit a pre-prepared interpretation. Whether or not this was the case, the thing to keep in mind is that it *is* possible to stretch a historical reading too far; the bottom line, as always, is that the text should be the starting point, leading towards particular readings, not the other way around.

(2) The concentration on history as context can overlook or downplay the aesthetic qualities of a text. Texts can be seen solely as historical artefacts, historical documents that are only valuable for the ways in which they interact with their times. There is a danger when reading a text through history that the critic reduces the text to the status of a historical product, just like any other, rather than seeing its individuality and uniqueness. This tendency is evident in Georg Lukács's broadly Marxist *The Meaning of Contemporary Realism* (1962), for example, which values realist novels largely for the ways in which they reinforce a Marxist worldview, as opposed to valuing them for their inherent artistic qualities. More experimental, modernist novels, are seen as politically detached in the way they focus on the internal and psychological struggles of the individual, and as such deemed less relevant to an understanding of social and political experience than classic realist novels, which appear to confront the harsh realities of everyday life more explicitly.

It was just such a limiting version of historical criticism that was eloquently dismissed by T. S. Eliot:

> We must not confuse knowledge – factual information – about a poet's period, the conditions of the society in which he lives, the ideas current in his time implicit in his writings, the state of the language in his period – with understanding his poetry. Such knowledge ... may be a necessary preparation for understanding the poetry; furthermore, it has a value of its own, as history; but for the appreciation of the poetry, it can only lead us to the door: we must find our own way in.[6]

(3) Not only does an effective historical reading of a text require good historical knowledge (historical knowledge that is more than simply a timeline of all the

'key' events of a period), but it requires careful and sophisticated handling. Just as was seen to be the case with the use of biographical information in Chapter 4, the onus is on the reader/critic to understand how history might 'work' for them and how historical information might be applicable. Thus, to make an assumption that because an author was writing during a period of war that their fiction must be *about* war in some way is likely to be misleading, underestimating the various ways in which people engage with and are affected by their historical circumstances.

To help you understand this point, ask yourself: If a reader/critic 100 years hence was to look back at the early twenty-first century and note that for a number of years the UK and US were involved in military conflict in the Middle East, how reasonable would it be for them to assume that *all* the texts produced during this period by writers from these two countries were in some way or other 'about' that ongoing conflict? This is the equivalent of the sort of sweeping assumptions some modern readers are willing to make about the relationship between text and history in past societies and cultures. It has become a critical 'wisdom', for example, to see texts written in the aftermath of the First World War as *inevitably* haunted by its presence. Such thinking is, if we think carefully about how societies operate and how particular events impact upon some people and not on others, deeply flawed.

Benefits of historical readings

(1) Reading texts in relation to their historical contexts offers the potential for sophisticated understandings of how cultures work. The variety of textual responses a culture offers to its social, political and economic circumstances is fascinating. To read texts in light of their historical circumstances sheds light on the backgrounds as much as it does on the texts themselves. It offers the reader a better way of understanding the past. For example, think of the different perspectives on the reform bills of 1832 and 1867 that are reflected in the tightly woven narrative web of George Eliot's *Middlemarch* (1872). Reading Eliot's novel historically allows the reader greater insight into the complex ways these specific historical changes impacted upon the lives of a variety of people. Just as Virginia Woolf's *Mrs Dalloway* (1925) connects the reader to the pervading sense of cultural depression during the 1920s that was part of the psychological impact of the Great War.

(2) The term 'history' is so broad that the examination of texts in terms of such a history allows the reader to expand their reading in almost limitless directions; they can look at the political history that informs the text, the military history, the social history, the intellectual history, etc. Which means that almost any aspect of a period can be made relevant to the reading, from psychological tracts, war plans, patterns of urban development, social habits, etc. This encourages multi-layered, interdisciplinary readings of texts that require

the reader to move beyond one-dimensional timelines of the historical past and towards a more sophisticated engagement in historical-contextual research. Thus, in enlightening *texts* the reader inevitably enlightens the *contexts* as well.

Creative exploration: history and contexts

It is sometimes difficult for modern readers to appreciate their own historical context. When we read work written within our own era we can be oblivious to some of the attitudes, ideologies, etc. that characterize the world around us. Similarly, when we read texts written in the past (and this *sense* of past-ness tends to increase in direct proportion to the distance between the past and our present) it is sometimes difficult to think beyond the obvious differences between our world and that past world. But it is important that this historical sense be developed, and finely tuned. So:

(1)   Select any *modern* text (the genre doesn't matter) that is set in the present day (or close to it). After reading this text, make some notes about the way in which the modern world is represented and how this 'history' has a role in the narrative/verse/drama.

(2)   The next stage is to identify an alternative historical setting; it need not necessarily be centuries distant, but it should be different enough that there are obvious points of contrast. Spend some time fleshing out a working knowledge and understanding of this alternative historical context; this will involve some research.

(3)   Identify a particular aspect of the original text (a particular passage, chapter, characterization, section of the plot, etc.). Rewrite this, setting it within your alternative historical context. This might require a significant amount of initial thought as to how things might alter/shift and what aspects need to be considered (that might not previously have been important) within this new version of the text.

(4)   The final stage, which is perhaps the most important part of the whole process, is for you to read back through your rewritten version of the original text and list what has changed. Some of the changes might be small, others will be very significant. The key is to try to understand what has changed across the two versions and why. When you complete the exercise you should be left with a clearer sense of the importance of the modern historical setting of the original text, which will be thrown into sharper relief by your rewritten version. The ultimate objective is for you to return to the original with a greater appreciation of its history and how this relates to the text as a whole.

Thinking about ... reading history

Are some texts more 'historical' than others? Give reasons for your answer.

Critical reading: History in Toni Morrison's *Beloved*

This section demonstrates how to use history as part of the reading of a text. In a way, it is about the seductiveness of such a reading – the way that *history* forces itself onto your attention even when you aren't particularly seeking it out. With specific reference to *Beloved*, the reading of the text will begin by deliberately *not* focusing on the historical context at all. However, as the reading develops it will be seen to very quickly require, demand even, additional knowledge about the historical context in order to satisfactorily consider different elements of the plot, characterization, setting and language.

Beloved without history

Beloved is a human tale of loss and bereavement written in a vivid, dramatic prose style: '124 was spiteful. Full of baby's venom. The women in the house knew it and so did the children.'[7] The character of Sethe is at the heart of the narrative. The sense of loss and absence that surrounds her is conjured up through the contrast between the one child she has with her as the novel begins (Denver, who is 18), the sons she has lost (who have gone) and the daughter who has died. By allowing the daughter to live on through the narrative (as a ghost, the reader discovers), Morrison emphasizes the contrast between what Sethe once had and the life she now leads. The melancholy of this is amplified with the arrival of the character of Paul D., who introduces the back history of Sethe and in particular the traumas of her past. Perhaps because of this shared traumatic history, Paul D. increasingly takes a hold over Sethe's life (and by implication that of Denver); he stands in an ambiguous relationship with the ominous 'schoolteacher' figure of Sethe's past, who lives on in the novel through memory.

By the time the relationship between Sethe and Paul D. is resurrected, there seems to have been a positive movement on Sethe's behalf from slavery to free choice – although this then gives way to a sense that Sethe has allowed herself to be taken over by Paul D., perhaps exchanging one form of slavery for another. Nevertheless, the theme of freedom recurs throughout the narrative and is central to Sethe's development as a female character in relation to the male figures around her. The complexity of the development is embodied in the contrast between Baby Suggs, who was emancipated but whose sons were sold, and Sethe, who is now free but struggling to disentangle herself from the past.

This outline of a potential reading of the text, noting some of the prevalent themes and patterns, suggests paths of interpretation that could easily be expanded upon. *However*, the opening epigraph/dedication of the novel, 'Sixty million or more', has been completely ignored so far in sketching out this largely non-contextual reading of the novel. And the reason for this is that it is a dedication that almost forces the reader of *Beloved* to confront the historical context of the novel from the outset. It requires the reader to make reference beyond the text for it to be decoded; only then is it possible to understand the quotation as an allusion to slavery and the dangerous 'passage' from Africa to North America of the slave ships, which resulted in hardship, disease and often death.

Beloved with history

But as soon as the reader allows this historical context into their consideration of the text, the power of much of the language and imagery of the novel takes on a greater significance: 'Dark ... I'm small in that place ... Hot. Nothing to breathe down there and no room to move' (p. 75). This can be seen as both an evocation of the womb of the mother and also of the recesses of the slave ship. The slaves were forced to live in dirty and cramped conditions in the lower quarters of these ships, where disease and ill-health were rife and food and water inadequate. Through such imagery the text insists that the reader consider the history of slavery, a lived history that haunts the characters in their present.

This sense of the historical past of the slaves and ex-slaves is apparent in the irony of Paul D. being freed by the Cherokee (evoking another element of America's colonial history), and the name of the character 'Stamp Paid', which he took for himself after he was forced to give up his wife to his master's son. *Beloved* continually confronts the reader with slave imagery and history, from Beloved's stream of consciousness (Ch. 22), to Sethe's eventual attack on the abolitionist Mr Bodwin (Ch. 27–8). The latter is carried out precisely (and ironically) *because* of the echoes of her slave past. This ongoing assertion of the importance of slave history culminates in the epilogue, with a return to the image of the baby in the womb, which this time really *is* a womb and not a slave ship, implying that the tragic history of the past is at last being escaped.

In the case of *Beloved*, even an outline reading of the novel quickly becomes enmeshed in considering the historical context and the ways in which its influence is felt through the language, dialogue and characterisation of the text. It is a difficult task to shape a reading that ignores the legacy of slavery, as this history weaves its way through almost every aspect of the narrative.

Having said that, there are other texts that do not evoke history so power-fully and so consistently; texts in which it is more feasible to overlook the specific historical context and instead to focus on a more isolated reading of the language, or a biographical reading, or a discussion of the text in relation to its literary history only. The key, for the developing reader, is to learn to understand when a historical reading is most appropriate – it is certainly possible to offer such a reading of *any* text, but you will gradually learn that some of these are more effective than others. In making the decision it is vital that you do so with a full appreciation of the strengths and weaknesses of such a reading. When you utilize history it can provide for exciting and dynamic readings, just as long as you are aware of the implications of doing so and the pitfalls along the way.

Checkpoint 4

To recap on the knowledge/skills you have gained in this chapter, consider the following questions (on your own at first, and then perhaps within seminars):

- How useful is historical knowledge in reading a text?
- How would you read a text if you didn't know when it was published or who its author was?
- What is lost if you consider a text only in terms of its historical context?
- How important is literary genre as a context for reading?
- On balance, do you favour a historical reading of texts? Why/why not?

Finally, produce a reading of *Beloved* that makes no mention/allusion to its historical context. Once completed, ask yourself whether there are any aspects of the text (other than slavery) that you particularly wanted to talk about but couldn't because that would rely on historical knowledge? What are the strengths of your non-historical reading?

Suggested further reading

Arnold, M., *Culture and Anarchy* (1869) – a lengthy consideration of the 'civilizing' powers of literature and culture.

Booker, C., *The Seven Basic Plots* (2004) – reductive but with an impressively wide frame of reference in terms of the 'types' of stories that have recurred across literary and cultural history.

Eliot, T. S., 'Tradition and the Individual Talent' (1919) – perhaps Eliot's most famous essay, enshrining the importance of literary history within the reading of texts.

Ellman, M., *Thinking About Women* (1968) – a landmark in feminist criticism.

Foucault, M., *Archaeology of Knowledge* (1972) – a key text in the evolving later twentieth-century consideration of representation, discourse and meaning.

—— *The Order of Things* (1970) – likewise.

—— *Discipline and Punish* (1975) – particularly focused on discourse of power, criminality and social Otherness.

—— *The History of Sexuality* (1976) – specifically concerned with social constructions of sexuality.

How to Read Texts

Frye, N., *Anatomy of Criticism* (1957) – an influential attempt to establish a 'science' of literary criticism.

Greenblatt, S., *Renaissance Self-fashioning: from More to Shakespeare* (1980) – the founding text of New Historicism.

Harris, M., *Cultural Materialism* (1979) – has a similar status in relation to Cultural Materialism.

Lukács, G., *The Meaning of Contemporary Realism* (1964) – Marxist analysis of the key differences between realism and modernism.

Millett, K., *Sexual Politics* (1969) – another founding text of feminist criticism.

Plato, *The Republic* (c. 360 BC) – a seminal text for a whole host of academic disciplines, including literary studies.

Propp, V., *The Morphology of the Folktale* (1958) – full of the structuralist analysis of narrative.

Said, E., *Orientalism* (1978) – a study of the Western construction of Eastern ('Oriental') identity, extremely influential on post-colonial criticism.

—— *Culture and Imperialism* (1993) – particularly insightful for its post-colonial 'revision' of the familiar texts of the Western canon, which are re-read in light of the experiences of colonized peoples.

Shelley, P. B., 'Preface' to *Prometheus Unbound* (1820) – one of a number of key critical works offered by Shelley in his attempt to justify the role and importance of the writer/artist/poet.

Showalter, E., *Toward a Feminist Poetics* (1979) – an important text in the Anglo-American feminist tradition.

Veeser, H. Aram (ed.), *The New Historicism* (1989) – contains a range of interesting essays that either account for, or fall within, the broad church that is New Historicism.

Stepping things up

Once you have completed all the exercises in this chapter and feel comfortable that you have absorbed the ideas, perspectives and approaches it has discussed, you are ready to engage in some more challenging work:

(1) What does 'The Man with the Twisted Lip' (which can be found in Appendix C) tell us about views of ethnicity in late Victorian society?

(2) How useful is 'The Man with the Twisted Lip' as an indicator of later nineteenth-century gender roles?

(3) Discuss the representation of 'knowledge' in 'The Man with the Twisted Lip'.

Critical theory

6

Chapter summary

This chapter will discuss the approaches to reading texts known as *critical* or *literary theory*, approaches that were in their various ways influenced by broader philosophical perspectives. Beginning with an introduction to the emergence of critical theory and some of the perspectives and assumptions that critical theories were reacting against, it will examine the impact of different critical-theoretical approaches. Towards the end of the chapter the discussion will consider how to deal with some of the complexities of critical theory through an initial reading of two philosophical essays and then through readings of Shakespeare's *Macbeth* (1603).

Thinking about ... philosophy and criticism

To begin your own process of considering how textual criticism can be informed by philosophical ideas and writings, spend some time thinking about how you could use the following extract as part of the process of reading a text.

> Capitalist production only really begins, as we have already seen, when each individual capitalist employs simultaneously a comparatively large number of labourers; when consequently the labour-process is carried on on an extensive scale and yields, relatively, large quantities of products. A greater number of labourers working together, at the same time, in one place (or, if you will, in the same field of labour), in order to produce the same sort of commodity under the mastership of one capitalist, constitutes, both historically and logically, the starting-point of capitalist production. With regard to the mode of production itself, manufacture, in its strict meaning, is hardly to be distinguished, in its earliest stages, from the handicraft trades of the guilds, otherwise than by the greater number of workmen simultaneously employed by one and the same individual capital. The workshop of the medieval master handicraftsman is simply enlarged.
>
> (from Karl Marx, *Capital*, volume 1, chapter 13 (1867))

Introduction

From the outset, one of the key objectives of *How to Read Texts* was to ensure that students were not too troubled by terms such as 'critical theory' or 'literary theory'. In looking at issues such as authorship, language, history and creativity, and considering how these issues were dealt with by different critical approaches, the idea has been to keep the discussion relatively free of abstract critical terminology or jargon. Which is why there has been a conscious effort made to weave a way through the range of critical approaches and skills (both historical and modern) without getting bogged down by ideas of 'critical theory' and 'literary theory', and to avoid much of the highly specialized language that has accompanied some theoretical approaches to reading. Instead, the idea has been to frame the chapters in relation to the possibilities of what can be achieved through different critical approaches, rooted in an appreciation of the various trends in criticism from the earliest times.

What is critical theory? A very short history

The terms 'critical theory' and 'literary theory' are more or less interchangeable. They imply types of criticism that were (in their own, often very different ways) founded in particular philosophical interpretations of history, society, culture, politics and individual identity. For this reason the approaches referred to by the terms 'critical theory' and 'literary theory' can also be understood as forms of 'philosophical theory'. Critics adopting or practising particular philosophical theories and approaches have tended to look at texts as source materials in relation to (for example) gender relations, psychological behaviours, economic conditions, the instability of language, etc. The move to 'theory' marked a shift away from critical approaches such as Practical and New Criticism, approaches that were more prone (although, as we have seen, not exclusively so) to viewing texts in isolation, separated from their historical circumstances.

That said, underpinning the reading of texts with an overarching philosophy was certainly not entirely new when 'theory' emerged in the twentieth century. T. S. Eliot claimed that this practice began with Coleridge: 'he established the relevance of philosophy, aesthetics and psychology; and once Coleridge had introduced these disciplines into literary criticism, future critics could ignore them only at their own risk.'[1] Yet, despite the fact that it is possible to trace the influence of philosophy on criticism prior to the twentieth century, the period of 'theory' was in truth one of unrivalled philosophical-critical activity, both in terms of the sheer volume of critical writing and also in the diversity and range of critical approaches. It was the period of (for example) Russian formalists, structuralists, narratologists, psychoanalysts, historicists (both old and new), Marxists, feminists, queer theorists, reader-response critics, post-colonialists, post-structuralists and the list goes on. All of these approaches to reading were rooted in specific philosophical positions, embodying particular ideas about knowledge, reality, interpretation, representation and being.

For example, the development of Freudian psychoanalysis in the later nineteenth century fed into specific forms of textual criticism in the later twentieth century that focused on the psychology of authors and the texts they created. And Marx's political philosophy of the mid-late nineteenth century eventually led to a critical consideration of the ways in which texts depicted the class tensions within them. Such relationships between textual criticism and trends in philosophical thinking were what most characterized the development of 'critical theory' in the twentieth century; whereas earlier examples of literary criticism had offered readers different and distinct ways of approaching texts, they tended to be more concerned with developing a method of reading than a philosophy of interpretation. Although the work of pre-theoretical critics certainly embodied ideological assumptions about writing, culture, and a range of other related issues, these tended to be less explicit within the criticism itself. As such, it is often much more difficult to identify a coherent, transparent, overarching framework of interpretation in earlier examples of critical practice.

Thinking about … philosophy and reading

What might be the difference between a *method of reading* and a *philosophy of interpretation*? Can you explain the difference between a *philosophical* and a *non-philosophical* reading of a text?

Ways of reading 'theory'

There is a range of books available that attempt to teach undergraduate students about 'theory' by analysing each critical approach in turn, working their way through what amounts to a 'check list' of the most popular theories. You will often find books with separate chapters on structuralism, post-structuralism and deconstruction, feminism, New Criticism, Marxism, New Historicism, post-colonialism, psychoanalysis, queer theory, reader-response criticism, etc. *How to Read Texts* (as hopefully you will have realized by now) is not one of those books. This is partly because, I believe, the label 'critical theory' can often be unhelpful, implying a coherent body of approaches to be learnt and applied, in some cases almost a critical doctrine to be absorbed, when in fact there are a wide variety of theories referred to by this term and many of them offer conflicting and even contradictory perspectives. To see these 'theories' as elements, perhaps filaments would be a better term, of a single coherent body of knowledge bears very little relation to the reality of how they actually evolved over time and how they have been applied over time.

As an undergraduate reader you cannot ignore the term 'critical theory'; it has a great prominence in criticism and maintains a high profile in university literature courses. But although you should not ignore the term, neither should you get too caught up in an unquestioning process of 'theory worship', wherein critical theories are seen as the only approaches to utilize as part of the reading of texts. The various critical theories should be explored, examined, and primarily *challenged*. You should not underestimate the ways in which 'critical theory' revolutionized the landscape of literary studies, asking a range of fundamental questions about history, society and culture, and politicizing and interrogating texts. However, at the same time you should understand that 'critical theory' amounts to just one particular phase in the history of literary criticism.

The 'what is literature?' debate

The truth of this last point, that it is important to view critical theory as a particular aspect of critical history rather than critical history in its entirety, is well illustrated by the debate surrounding the question 'what is literature?' For this debate, although significantly revitalized during the later twentieth century (what we might identify as the key period of critical theory), in fact has a far-reaching critical history. As such, the critical-theoretical phase of the debate is only part of the whole story.

Critical theory and 'literature'

Having said that, it would be churlish to deny that the emergence of 'critical theory' in the twentieth century was responsible for the many ways in which ideas of literature have become fundamentally contested and revised, perhaps forever undermining the notion of a coherent, elitist 'canon' of the supposedly best texts that should be taught and learnt. There were feminist critics who refused to accept that literary history should privilege dead white male writers, post-colonial critics who rejected what they saw as the whiteness of the 'canon', and Marxist critics who advocated the inclusive study of popular cultural texts instead of just those defined as 'literary'. All of which meant that although the idea of 'the canon' was still in evidence in the way schools and colleges (and examination boards) prescribed certain authors and texts (Shakespeare being a case in point), in the universities there was, in the later twentieth century, an increasing willingness to widen the range of texts that students could study.

'Literature' before theory: classical ideas

However, despite the undoubted significance of critical theory in terms of the question 'what is literature?', the origins of the debate take us back to Plato (which has been a recurring theme of *How to Read Texts*). For him, it was possible to define the 'best' texts as they were the ones with particular moral qualities:

they [writers] have said that unjust men are often happy, and just men
wretched, that wrong-doing pays if you can avoid being found out, and
that justice is what is good for someone else but is to your own advantage. We must forbid them to say this sort of thing, and require their
poems and stories to have quite the opposite moral.[2]

This moral dimension was linked to the specific *forms* of writing, and writers
were to use the form as the vehicle for their moral purpose: 'Poetry and fiction
fall into three classes. First, that which employs representation only, tragedy and
comedy, as you say. Secondly, that in which the poet speaks in his own person;
the best example is lyric poetry. Thirdly, that which employs both methods, epic
and various other kinds of poetry' (p. 152).

For Aristotle, following on from Plato, it was important to value texts that
combined *realism* with morality: 'like the painter or any other artist, the poet
aims at the representation of life; necessarily, therefore, he must always represent
things in one of three ways: either as they were or are, or as they are said to be
or seem to be, or as they ought to be.'[3] Aristotle's definition of the highest form
of writing also took account of the effect texts had on an audience's emotions,
which explained his interest in tragedy as a form, as the success of tragedy
was defined in terms of the ways in which it affected its audience. For him
the depiction of character and plot were key in this, and if tragic drama was
successful then the audience would be moved to experience emotion, 'by means
of pity and fear bringing about the purgation of such emotions' (p. 39). This was
the idea of 'catharsis', wherein the highest forms of writing incited an emotional
outpouring from the audience by encouraging them to identity with characters
and their plights.

Horace, the Roman critic and poet, defined in his *Ars Poetica* ('On the Art of
Poetry' (c.13 BC)) the best poetic writing as that which was 'sweet and useful'.
For him it was important that writers chose their subject and form carefully:
'give long thought to what you are capable of undertaking, and what is beyond
you.'[4] The 'experienced poet' or 'imitative artist' was required to 'look to human
life and character for his models, and from them derive a language that is true to
life' (p. 90). This was what marked out the highest forms of expression. There was
no room for detachment or aloofness, poets had to 'aim at giving either profit
or delight, or at combining the giving of pleasure with some useful precepts for
life' (p. 90). This echoes with the Platonic sense of poetry as something which
positively contributed to the society from which it emerged.

In his 'On the Sublime', the Greek critic Longinus (1st century AD) defined
poetry as writing that contained a greater sense of grandeur, seeing it as inspired
by the voice of God: 'sublimity consists in a certain excellence and distinction in
expression ... it is from this source alone that the greatest poets and historians
have acquired their pre-eminence and won for themselves an eternity of fame.'[5]
The poet, as a consequence, was to adopt 'elevated language' intended 'not to

persuade the hearer' but 'to entrance them', language which 'transports us with wonder' (p. 100). Poetry was not a mere 'impression of grandeur', but sublime writing that caused the reader to be 'filled with a proud exaltation and a sense of vaunting joy, just as though we had ourselves produced what we had heard' (p. 107). Poetry was not to be simply moral, but also spiritual as well, with the power and potential to provoke religious responses in its audience.

'Literature' before theory: English letters

Sir Philip Sidney (most notably in his *A Defence of Poetry* (1595)), one of the leading Elizabethan critics, defined poetic writing as that which lifted the hearts and emotions of the readers. Great literary works were distinguished from other forms of writing for the way in which they gave their readers a deeper pleasure: 'Poesy therefore is an art of imitation ... that is to say, a representation, counterfeiting, or figuring forth – to speak metaphorically, a speaking picture – with this end, to teach and delight.'[6] Sidney defined three types of poetry: divine poetry which 'did imitate the unconceivable excellencies of God' (p. 25), poetry that dealt 'with matters philosophical, either moral ... or natural ... or astronomical ... or historical' (p. 26), and poetry that attempted to 'teach and delight' by focusing 'with learned discretion, into the divine consideration of what may be and should be' (p. 26). What each of these shared was a power to: 'move men to take that goodness in hand, which without delight they would fly as from a stranger; and teach, to make them know that goodness whereunto they are moved' (p. 27).

Samuel Johnson, on the other hand, was less concerned with the moral and spiritual dimensions of writing and more with its aesthetic qualities. Of the work of George Stepney it was remarked, for example: 'in his original poems, now and then, a happy line may perhaps be found, and now and then a short composition may give pleasure; but there is, in the whole, little either of the grace of wit, or the vigour of nature.'[7] And although Johnson did not explain or elaborate upon what he meant by terms such as 'grace', 'wit', or 'the vigour of nature', it was apparent that for him he was judging Stepney's work on the basis of specific 'known' artistic criteria. He just assumed that these were unarguable and uncontested. This is similarly the case with Johnson's criticism of the devotional poetry of Isaac Watts, about which he wrote: '[It is] ... like that of others, unsatisfactory. The paucity of its topics enforces perpetual repetition, and the sanctity of the matter rejects the ornaments of figurative diction.'[8]

'Literature' before theory: the Romantics

The period of the Romantic poets in England, which ran from the later eighteenth century through until the end of the Georgian era, was one of fevered debate in terms of the definition and explication of the highest forms of writing. William Wordsworth (1770–1850) was central to this debate, offering as he did a radical new manifesto as to the nature of true poetic writing. For him, poets were to strive for originality, human emotion, and imagination. Wordsworth saw artistic expression as being about the celebration of ordinary lives, expressed through language that was not artificial or grand. In the 'advertisement' to his *Lyrical Ballads*, for example, Wordsworth identified his poems as 'experiments', written to see 'how far the language of conversation in the middle and lower classes of society is adapted to the purposes of poetic pleasure'.[9] This was a radical and challenging statement of poetic purpose, recognizing that some readers 'will perhaps frequently have to struggle with feelings of strangeness and awkwardness' (p. 166) because Wordsworth's writing did not conform to their own inherited notions of what poetry was.

This attempt to redefine the nature of poetic and literary expression was further delineated in Wordsworth's later 'preface' to the 1802 edition of the *Lyrical Ballads*. This offered a definition of poetry as 'fitting to metrical arrangement a selection of the real language of men in a state of vivid sensation'.[10] Wordsworth was trying to provoke 'feelings of strangeness and awkwardness' in readers as they read 'incidents and situations from common life ... in a language really used by men' (p. 252). This focus on the everyday and the ordinary was deliberate, and accorded with his broad aims as a poet: 'low and rustic life was generally chosen because in that condition the essential passions of the heart find a better soil in which they can attain their maturity, are less under restraint' (p. 252). Wordsworth 'proposed to myself to imitate – and as far as is possible, to adopt – the very language of men', wishing 'to keep my reader in the company of flesh and blood' (p. 255).

Perhaps most famously, Wordsworth defined the poet as: 'a man speaking to men – a man (it is true) endued with more lively sensibility, more enthusiasm and tenderness, who has a greater knowledge of human nature, and a more comprehensive soul, than are supposed to be common among mankind' (p. 257). Poetry was as a consequence seen as 'the spontaneous overflow of powerful feelings' which were then shaped and moderated by the poet, a process captured in the phrase 'emotion recollected in tranquillity' (p. 263).

Coleridge, the long-time creative partner of Wordsworth, identified the highest forms of writing as those that achieved a perfect balance between instinctive, emotional qualities and deliberate, rational ones:

> as the *elements* of metre owe their existence to a state of increased excitement, so the metre itself should be accompanied by the natural language of excitement ... as these elements are formed into metre *artificially*, by a *voluntary* act, with the design and for the purpose of blending *delight* with emotion, so the traces of present *volition* should throughout the metrical language be proportionally discernible. Now these two conditions must be reconciled and co-present. There must be not only a partnership, but a union; an interpenetration of passion and of will, of *spontaneous* impulse and *voluntary* purpose.[11]

How to Read Texts

It was the role of the poet/writer to create texts that displayed a harmony between thought, feeling and artistic application, wherein form and language were not isolated from the creative instincts that gave life to the work in the first instance, but were the lifeblood of these instincts.

Shelley's idea of poetry, although radical in its own way, was clearly influenced by the critical thinkers that preceded him, including Plato, Aristotle, Horace and Sidney. For Shelley celebrated both the role of poetry and the status of the poet: 'poetry turns all things to loveliness; it exalts the beauty of that which is most beautiful and it adds beauty to that which is most deformed; it marries exultation and horror, grief and pleasure, eternity and change; it subdues to union, under its light yoke, all irreconcilable things'.[12] At the same time, he acknowledged that the poet was 'the author to others of the highest wisdom, pleasure, virtue, and glory, so he ought personally to be the happiest, the best, the wisest, and the most illustrious of men' (p. 295). For Shelley it was 'the business of the poet to communicate to others the pleasure and the enthusiasm arising out of those images and feelings in the vivid presence of which within his own mind consists at once his inspiration and his reward'.[13] The poetry he created was, as he noted in 'A Defence of Poetry', a combination of 'new materials of knowledge, and power, and pleasure', arranged 'according to a certain rhythm and order' (p. 293).

'Literature' before theory: modernists and afterwards

In the early twentieth century there was a shift away from the Romantic idea of poetic writing as an original and 'spontaneous overflow' of emotion. T. S. Eliot, for one, defined literature as the combination of tradition and originality. The highest forms of writing were seen as having been influenced by the best work of the writers of the past, whilst at the same time offering their own contribution to literary history:

> One of the facts that might come to light ... is our tendency to insist, when we praise a poet, upon those aspects of his work in which he least resembles anyone else ... Whereas if we approach a poet without this prejudice we shall often find that not only the best, but the most individual parts of his work may be those in which the dead poets, his ancestors, assert their immortality most vigorously.[14]

However, the influence of past writers was not to detract from the originality of the work, which was to be characterized by the exclusion of the life and personality of the author. Eliot talked of the 'continual surrender' of the self in literary writing, of a 'continual self-sacrifice ... [a] continual extinction of personality' (p. 28). There had to be an evident sense of the poet writing themselves out of their work: 'not a turning loose of emotion, but an escape from emotion; it [literature] is not the expression of personality, but an escape from personality'

(p. 34). This was a reversal of Wordsworth's view of poetry, marking the divergence between Romantic and early twentieth-century modernist ideas.

After Eliot, and with the development of critical theory in the later twentieth century, the debate about 'what is literature?' became more overtly politicized. The status of high art versus popular texts was considered, as well as the different ways in which the term 'literature' has been loaded in terms of particular assumptions about ethnicity, social class, gender and race. 'Literature' thus became a site of struggle between competing political and philosophical interests.

Thinking about ... literature

What is at stake in the decision as to what is, and what is not, 'literature'?

The effects of theory

In the 1980s and early 1990s there were heated debates about the value and importance of critical theory in universities all over the world. Some institutions became 'theoretical' fairly quickly, others took much longer to accept that critical theory was a key aspect of the modern study of texts. In the early twenty-first century, some universities are stoically sticking to their commitment to critical theory as the most effective and desirable way to read texts. Others, on the other hand, are starting to move away from the systematic study of critical theories, marking a shift towards what has been called *post-theory* – criticism that is certainly influenced by the developments of 'theory', but which at the same time looks to combine or else work beyond the boundaries of the various critical 'schools'.

How to Read Texts should be seen within this context of a re-appraisal of the nature of textual criticism. Critical theories have not been privileged as the *only* ways of unlocking texts, and reader/critics have been encouraged to develop their own individual critical voices, drawing on and influenced by a range of methods and approaches from both past and present. Yet, it is also true to say that many of the underlying ideas about reading in *How to Read Texts* have been informed by the developments and assumptions of critical theory. Such as:

- The role of the reader in the construction of textual meaning is assumed as fundamental. The balance of the discussion has been towards a recognition of the fact that the role of the reader cannot be ignored.
- The notion that there is a single 'correct' reading of a text has been rejected. Within the chapters of this book the overarching idea has been that meaning is multiple and subjective.
- Human identity (ethnicity, gender, social class, etc.) has been viewed

throughout *How to Read Texts* as complex, often unstable and under continuous challenge. And the *representation* of this identity has been seen as contradictory and in tension. There is an inherent assumption against absolute notions of identity (such as the idea of a universal human nature), even though the popularity and pervasiveness of such notions has been recognized, and readers have been given licence to make up their own minds about this.

- The idea that all criticism and textual analysis is political, and has a relationship with ideology, is acknowledged. In particular, much of the discussion in the various chapters has been founded in the idea that there is no objective, value-free position from which to read texts.

The achievements of theory

All of which means that even those who see critical theory as a 'moment' in a much longer history of criticism, and not as a lens through which all texts must be read, have to concede that the theoretical developments of the twentieth century, and the impact of these on the study of texts, have been very significant. Much of the criticism during the period of 'critical theory' has been insightful, lucid and thought-provoking. Even if, at the same time, we have to accept that there have also been examples of theoretical criticism that were not just philosophically complicated but at times opaque in terms of the language they used and the almost jargonistic way in which they attempted to convey their ideas and key concepts.

Approaching theoretical criticism: a way through the maze

The philosophical complexity of some critical theory and the tendency of some critical-theoretical writing to use (perhaps unnecessarily) complex language, technical terms, or concepts that take a great deal of deciphering, present a particular challenge for undergraduate students. Furthermore, many of the critical writings that students come across as they familiarize themselves with 'theory' do not contain any explicit method for reading texts, and are primarily philosophical rather than literary-critical works. They require a sophisticated interpretation in order to make them applicable as part of textual readings. Which means that the challenge these works present to students is twofold; first, to understand and interpret sophisticated primary material, and second, to apply this understanding and interpretation in a way that can provide the basis for the reading of a text.

Take, for example, the area of critical study known as 'French feminism'. Emerging in the 1970s, but largely separate from the Anglo-American methods of feminist critique that emerged at the same time, French feminism was more explicitly philosophical, theoretical even, that its Anglo-American cousin, influenced as it was by thinkers such as Hegel, Heidegger and Jean-Paul Sartre, and especially by post-structuralists including Jacques Derrida. French feminists were also fundamentally influenced by psychoanalysis, not just that of Sigmund Freud (1856–1939) but also (and perhaps in a sense even more so) the work of Freud's disciple Jacques Lacan (1901–81).

French feminist criticism was as such notable for the way in which it was written in language that was often complex, eccentric, metaphorical and rich in symbolism. Take the following as an example:

> Writing has been run by a libidinal and cultural – hence political, typically masculine – economy; that this is a locus where the repression of women has been perpetuated, over and over, more or less consciously, and in a manner that's frightening since it's often hidden or adorned with the mystifying charms of fiction; that this locus has grossly exaggerated all the signs of sexual opposition (and not sexual difference), where woman has never her turn to speak – this being all the more serious and unpardonable in that writing is the very possibility of change, the space that can serve as a spring board for subversive thought, the precursory movement of a transformation of social and cultural structures.
>
> (from Hélène Cixous, 'The Laugh of the Medusa' (1975))

Yet, despite the challenges presented by such philosophically complex forms of criticism, it is important that students developing their skills of textual reading immerse themselves in these primary materials. It is perfectly fine to begin by using one of the many available introductory guide-books to acclimatize you to the complexities of critical theory in a user-friendly way, but before too long it will become imperative that you make a concerted attempt to engage with the original philosophical/theoretical writings themselves, and to learn how to work with these as a stage in your critical development.

And the reason for this is simple. Any secondary explanation of or introduction to critical theory is in itself an *interpretation*. It is individual, subjective and by definition partial. Elements of the original theory have been selected and highlighted in the light of the author's own experience, interests and presuppositions. In a helpful student guide, moreover, there has to be an element of simplification – not only has the author interpreted the original material, they have worked hard (we would hope) to make it as digestible as possible to the reader. Some authors of such introductory books show great skill in relaying complex material in a simple and straightforward way, but the bottom line is that this process of reinterpretation is not going to be as detailed or as philosophically complex as the original critical essays. This is why it is important as an apprentice critic to persevere with material that might, at first look, seem beyond you. Even if, after much perseverance, you still feel a little like this, the effort exerted will not have been wasted and you will have learnt more than you appreciate. Even if you only manage to identify a few usable ideas or concepts out of the mass of material you have read, this is still a worthwhile process.

....

Thinking about ... the challenge of theory

Why do you think that some readers find 'theory' difficult to read and understand? Consider the Cixous extract (above) as part of your answer.

....

In order to show how the process of coming to terms with difficult philosophical/theoretical material can work, much of the remainder of this chapter will focus on two specific philosophical essays. These are essays that do not straightforwardly lend themselves to the reading of texts, as they are more broadly philosophical than literary-critical. Which means that rather than applying an already established and ready-made approach to reading, we have to establish a basis for reading for ourselves from the original essays.

The intention is thus to read Sigmund Freud's 'Civilization and its Discontents' (1930) and Teresa de Lauretis's 'Upping the Anti [sic] in Feminist Theory' (1990)[15] in terms of their philosophical ideas, and establishing their key points.

NB. You will at this point need to obtain copies of both these essays to use as the basis of your reading/interpretation.

Once this has been done we can begin to apply some of the central ideas to the question of how to read a text and to the development of an outline literary-critical method. The two essays have been selected because they are clearly philosophical without being specifically literary-critical and because they contain sophisticated ideas and at times complex language that require some effort on the part of the reader to come to terms with.

Reading theory 1: Freud, 'Civilization and its Discontents'

The first stage of handling philosophical material such as this should be a fairly superficial read-through of the whole piece (in one sitting if it is a short essay, section by section if it is a longer work). At this stage you need take no notes beyond some general headings to provide you with a 'map' of the piece. What you are looking for is a general sense of how it hangs together, what its key themes are and which parts are more or less difficult. One of the main reasons for doing this is that some examples of philosophical criticism are so intellectually dense, requiring such an effort of thought, that by the time you get to the end (if you haven't mapped out the piece in the first instance) you have little or no sense of what the overarching themes and points were.

So, when attempting a read-through of the Freud piece a reader might break it down (in terms of its sections/movements of argument) like this:

- How people measure value in life (both accurately and falsely).
- The nature of religious feeling.
- How this links to the ego and its relationship with the external world.
- The way a past mental life can be relevant to the present.
- Parallels between the psychological effects of art and the psychological effects of religion.
- The enriching (psychological) effects of culture.
- The need for the imagination to be stimulated and for beauty to be enjoyed if happiness is to be achieved.
- The ways in which present civilization is *not* bringing about such enjoyment.
- Modern civilization is seen in opposition with the path of 'love' and the desires of the 'libido'.
- Neurosis, anxiety and guilt are identified as the consequence of this tension between 'love' and 'libido'.
- The question is posed as to whether cultural development can alleviate the problems caused by society's dysfunctional instincts of aggression and self-destruction.

Once this initial 'mapping' of the essay is complete, the next stage is for you to go through the piece again but this time in much more detail. It will be necessary to take more notes, quote from key sections, and make sure that as you go through you pause to clarify what exactly the argument is at each stage.

Thinking about ... Freud

As an example of how this more detailed reading works, read through the following extract, trying to establish as much useful knowledge as you can:

> I believe the line of thought which seeks to trace in the phenomena of cultural development the part played by a super-ego promises still further discoveries. I hasten to come to a close. But there is one question which I can hardly evade. If the development of civilization has such a far-reaching similarity to the development of the individual and if it employs the same methods; may we not be justified in reaching the diagnosis that, under the influence of cultural urges, some civilizations, or some epochs of civilization – possibly the whole of mankind – have become 'neurotic'? An analytic dissection of such neuroses might lead to therapeutic recommendations which could lay claim to great practical interest. I would not say that an attempt of this kind to carry

psycho-analysis over to the cultural community was absurd or doomed to be fruitless. But we should have to be very cautious and not forget that, after all, we are only dealing with analogies and that it is dangerous, not only with men but also with concepts, to tear them from the sphere in which they have originated and been evolved. Moreover, the diagnosis of communal neuroses is faced with a special difficulty. In an individual neurosis we take as our starting-point the contrast that distinguishes the patient from his environment, which is assumed to be 'normal'. For a group all of whose members are affected by one and the same disorder no such background could exist; it would have to be found elsewhere. And as regards the therapeutic application of our knowledge, what would be the use of the most correct analysis of social neuroses, since no one possesses authority to impose such a therapy upon the group? But in spite of all these difficulties, we may expect that one day someone will venture to embark upon a pathology of cultural communities.[16]

Once you have finished working on the first extract from the Freud essay, move on to the next, trying to identify the ideas and concepts that can be seen as of most relevance to the practice of reading texts:

For a wide variety of reasons, it is very far from my intention to express an opinion upon the value of human civilization. I have endeavoured to guard myself against the enthusiastic prejudice which holds that our civilization is the most precious thing that we possess or could acquire and that its path will necessarily lead to heights of unimagined perfection. I can at least listen without indignation to the critic who is of the opinion that when one surveys the aims of cultural endeavour and the means it employs, one is bound to come to the conclusion that the whole effort is not worth the trouble, and that the outcome of it can only be a state of affairs which the individual will be unable to tolerate. My impartiality is made all the easier to me by my knowing very little about all these things. One thing only do I know for certain and that is that man's judgements of value follow directly his wishes for happiness – that, accordingly, they are an attempt to support his illusions with arguments. (p. 771)

There are many aspects that you *could* have commented on across both of these extracts from the Freud essay. These *might* include:

- the role of the super-ego (the conscience, effectively) in the way in which 'culture' develops
- the ways in which some civilizations can become 'neurotic' (plagued by fundamental anxieties)
- the possibility that these civilizations can be subjected to psychoanalysis in order to help them overcome their neuroses
- the question as to whether 'civilization' is wholly and always a positive thing

- Freud's claim to be free from bias or subjectivity (achieving what he calls 'impartiality')
- the tendency of men to value most what makes them happy ('to support his illusions with arguments').

When we begin to develop readings of *Macbeth*, below, we will decide which of these aspects to focus on in particular.

Reading theory 2: de Lauretis, 'Upping the Anti [sic] in Feminist Theory'

Begin by reading through this essay and offering your own outline 'mapping' of the key ideas. This will include (at least some of) the ways in which it:

- Introduces the term 'essentialism'.
- Defines 'essential' differences between different feminist positions.
- Sees human essence as the 'triangle' of properties/qualities/attributes.
- Questions the idea that all women share a common experience.
- Identifies 'radical-liberal' versions of feminism, such as those focusing on black and lesbian experience.
- Highlights the contradictions within post-structuralist feminism concerning their advocacy of a female essence.
- Attempts to reconcile these contradictions by looking back at the history of feminist thought since the 1970s.
- Argues for the idea of the 'female-embodied social subject' as the resolution of many of the inner tensions and contradictions within feminist thinking in relation to ideas of 'essence'.

Once you have 'mapped' the essay for yourself, the next stage is to consider it in greater detail.

Thinking about ... de Lauretis

Analyse the following extract:

> Nowadays, the term *essentialism* covers a range of metacritical meanings and strategic uses that go the very short distance from convenient label to buzzword. Many who, like myself, have been involved with feminist critical theory for some time and who did use the term, initially, as a serious critical concept, have grown impatient with this word – essentialism – time and again repeated with its reductive ring, its self-righteous tone of superiority, its contempt for 'them' – those guilty of it. Yet, few would deny that feminist theory is all about an essential difference, an irreducible difference, though not a difference between woman

and man, nor a difference inherent in 'woman's nature' (in woman as nature), but a difference in the feminist conception of woman, women, and the world.

Let us say, then, that there is an essential difference between a feminist and a non-feminist understanding of the subject and its relation to institutions; between feminist and non-feminist knowledges, discourses and practices of cultural forms, social relations, and subjective processes; between a feminist and a non-feminist historical consciousness. That difference is essential in that it is constitutive of feminist thinking and thus of feminism: it is what makes the thinking feminist, and what constitutes certain ways of thinking, certain practices of writing, reading, imaging, relating, acting, etc., into the historically diverse and culturally heterogeneous social movement which, qualifiers and distinctions notwithstanding, we continue with good reasons to call feminism. Another way to say this is that the essential difference of feminism lies in its historical specificity – the particular conditions of its emergence and development, which have shaped its object and field of analysis, its assumptions and forms of address; the constraints that have attended its conceptual and methodological struggles; the erotic component of its political self-awareness; the absolute novelty of its radical challenge to social life itself.[17]

A close consideration of this passage might draw particular attention to:

- the meaningfulness of the term 'essentialism' and the ways it has been used and (supposedly) misused in the past
- the idea that feminist approaches, in their different ways, have all been about 'essential difference', particularly in the ways that these approaches have understood the world and women's roles within it
- the view that feminist philosophy and criticism is 'essentially' different from all other forms of philosophy and criticism, partly at least because of the different historical circumstances that it emerged out of
- the way in which feminism is defined as both politically self-aware and radical.

Now, once you have considered this extract, and the essay as a whole, in detail, the next step is for you to embark upon initial readings of Shakespeare's *Macbeth*, based on what has emerged from your work on the Freud and de Lauretis criticism.

Critical reading: Shakespeare's *Macbeth*

Psychoanalytic criticism

Our initial outline *psychoanalytic* reading of *Macbeth* needs to begin by considering which aspects of Freud's 'Civilization and its Discontents' are most useful to us in reading the text. This will grow out of our work on the selected passages from the essay, which flagged up (among others) issues to do with the relationship between human conscience and how 'culture' develops, the ways in which some civilizations can become plagued by anxieties, the possibility that civilizations can be subjected to psychoanalysis in order to help them overcome their neuroses, the question whether being 'civilized' is always a positive thing, the idea that the psychoanalyst can be impartial, and the tendency of men to confuse 'value' with 'desire'.

For the purposes of this initial consideration of Shakespeare's play, two of these aspects will be considered in reading the text:

(1) the idea of civilization as plagued by neuroses, making it open to psychoanalytic interpretation
and
(2) the confusion between value and desire.

So, here goes:

(1) *Macbeth* begins, symbolically, with thunder, lightning and three witches. The scene is an omen, indicating disquiet and unease. The contradiction of 'fair is foul, and foul is fair' (Act I, Scene i) indicates a society within which things are turned on their head. And yet, the very next scene of the play, set in 'a camp', indicates a hierarchical world of honour and duty: 'O valiant cousin! Worthy gentleman!' (Act I, Scene ii).

What Shakespeare thus achieves in these first two scenes is a representation of a society that appears on the outside to be at ease with itself, to be confident and secure, but on the inside this society is enmeshed in tensions and personal jealousies. The fact that the hero Macbeth is seduced so quickly into disloyalty against his beloved monarch implies that all was not well in the first place, and that what had appeared to be a harmonious and civilized world was rooted in insecurity. The Freudian sense of the neurosis of civilization is relevant here, where the surface (conscious) level of society appears untroubled and stable, and yet at a deeper (unconscious) level anxieties and potentially destructive desires predominate. This is embodied in the means by which Macbeth becomes Thane of Cawdor, which occurs only after the disgrace of the previous Thane ('that most disloyal traitor' (Act

I, Scene iii)), who assisted the King of Norway in battle against Duncan's army in a bid to further his own personal-political interests.

(2)   In the early parts of *Macbeth*, Freud's suggestion that men have a tendency to value most what makes them happy (and convince themselves that because they desire something it must be valuable) is supported by Macbeth's initial responses to the witches' prophecy: 'Stars, hide your fires; let not light see my black and deep desires' (Act I, Scene v). He is 'rapt in the wonder' (Act I, Scene v) in thinking that he will receive greater honours, and possibly even the greatest of all honours in becoming King. There is a clear sense that he has been beguiled by these suggestions of advancement, and the idea that he has been fated for true greatness. His desire for the prophecy to come true convinces him that greater titles and influence are important, and he values them precisely *because* he convinces himself that this is what he really wants.

   However, as the play unfolds this Freudian sense of the relationship between 'value' and 'desire' breaks down. The character of Macbeth becomes increasingly aware of the tension between what he thought he most wanted (influence, political power, and ultimately the throne) and the reality of how he achieved these things. The position that he achieves is almost entirely diminished by the fact that he usurped the crown from Duncan. Macbeth becomes aware that the true value of something, in this case the throne, is not the same as the extent of a person's desire for it. Simply to want the throne with a great passion does not make it, in itself, inevitably valuable. The real worth of the throne, he realizes too late, is compromised because the succession is not legally valid, and his ambition has come to nothing. This sense of realization is captured towards the end of the play:

> Tomorrow, and tomorrow, and tomorrow
> Creeps in this petty pace from day to day,
> To the last syllable of recorded time:
> And all our yesterdays have lighted fools
> The way to dusty death. Out, out, brief candle!
> Life's but a walking shadow, a poor player
> That struts and frets his hour upon the stage
> And then is heard no more. It is a tale
> Told by an idiot, full of sound and fury
> Signifying nothing. (Act V, Scene v)

Feminist criticism

In developing our outline *feminist* reading of *Macbeth*, based on our analysis of 'Upping the Anti [sic] in Feminist Theory', again we have to consider which aspects of the essay to make use of. This will include at least some of: the meaningfulness of the term 'essentialism', the idea that feminism is always about 'essential difference', the view that feminist approaches are 'essentially' different from all other critical approaches, and the notion of feminism as both politically self-aware and radical.

For the purposes of this initial reading, we will look at the idea of 'essentialism', and in particular the question whether men and women are essentially different, in relation to two aspects of *Macbeth*:

(1) The characterization of Macbeth himself
(2) The role of Lady Macbeth.

(1) Macbeth begins the play as a great man, loved and respected by his people and his king. He is defined by the text as the quintessential hero-figure:

> For brave Macbeth – well he deserves that name –
> Disdaining Fortune, with his brandished steel,
> Which smoked with bloody execution,
> Like valor's minion carved out his passage
> Till he faced the slave;
> Which nev'r shook hand, nor bade farewell to him,
> Till he unseamed him from the nave to th' chops,
> And fixed his head upon our battlements. (Act I, Scene ii)

His first reaction on being told by the three witches that his future might be even grander than that of a hero of battle (Thane of Glamis, then Thane of Cawdor, then ultimately 'King hereafter' (Act I, Scene ii)) is to question the prophecy: 'Say from whence you owe this strange intelligence?' (Act I, Scene iii). He is intrigued when he first writes to his wife, but he does not believe the prophecy. Throughout the period leading up to the murder of King Duncan, Macbeth seems lacking in the 'qualities' of a murderer, but there is still a tension between the heroic masculinity of the early moments of the play, his code of honour in battle, and his behaviour beyond the context of war. His wife questions his ambition and asks whether he has the courage to realize his political aspirations: 'Your hand, your tongue: look like th' innocent flower, but be the serpent under 't' (Act I, Scene v). This suggests a weaknesses in his character (as far as she is concerned), leading him to be dominated by his wife, who herself displays more stereotypically masculine characteristics (ruthlessness, ambition, threats of violence). Lady Macbeth attempts to provoke him into a more masculine form of behaviour: 'When you durst do it, then you were a man; and to be more than what you were, you would be so much more the man' (Act I, Scene vii).

After he becomes king, a pinnacle of male achievement during his historical era, Macbeth is psychologically tortured by what he has done to gain the throne.

He is haunted by visions (e.g. of Banquo), and this mental disturbance pushes him into yet greater barbarism (including the murder of Macduff's family). After the death of his own wife, Macbeth falls into a deep depression and melancholy, which culminates in his own death at the hands of Macduff. The play provides the reader with a gradual questioning of the true nature of the hero Macbeth was during the early part of the play, doubting whether he was *essentially* the person he appeared to be, and suggesting that perhaps his initial reputation was undeserved.

(2) This questioning of the essence of Macbeth is paralleled in the way in which Lady Macbeth is represented. Because from the first it is clear that her ambitious vision for her husband does not fit easily with stereotypical ideas of female/feminine behaviour. She shows none of the doubts and hesitations that her husband displays, and is the driving force behind the plot to kill King Duncan. When Macbeth arrives at Inverness it becomes clear that his wife is determined that he carry out the plan, and she overcomes his doubts. In effect, she adopts the more masculine role, with the power of the relationship mostly on her side, forcing the reader to question not just who Lady Macbeth really is, but whether the female stereotype of passivity and propriety has any basis in reality (at least as far as she is concerned).

Having said that, in the aftermath of the murder Lady Macbeth experiences psychological breakdown, becoming tormented in her sleep and hallucinating during the day. She is haunted by the bloodstains on her hands until the point where, ultimately, she commits suicide. This aspect of her personality more closely fits the historical stereotype of women as more susceptible to mental fragility and breakdown, which has particularly been associated with women who are not mothers. The patriarchal idea was that somehow women were not 'essential' women until they had given birth to children, and that as a consequence they were more prone to mental imbalance or deviant forms of behaviour.

These initial readings of *Macbeth*, one broadly psychoanalytic and one broadly feminist, are intended to help you better understand the process of developing theoretically informed textual readings of your own. They are a starting point for your own analysis of Shakespeare's play, as well as illustrations of how you might begin to read other texts using similar critical methods. Ultimately, the idea is that you become comfortable with a wide range of different critical-theoretical material and learn to read and decipher this as the basis for the development of your own theoretically informed critical method.

Checkpoint 5

To test the knowledge you have gained in this chapter, consider the following questions:

- To what extent is theory inevitable? Is there a way of reading texts that is not theoretical?
- Read at least one primary theoretical essay and examine its assumptions and approach. 'Map' this out before reading it in detail.
- Offer a reading of *Macbeth* that grows out of your reading of this theoretical essay.
- Develop an alternative reading of Shakespeare's play, one that you regard to be un-theoretical or less theoretical than the first. Ask yourself, and indeed your fellow students in seminars, about the strengths and weaknesses of both of these readings.

Creative exploration: critical theory

The creative exercise below is designed to further your empathy and appreciation of some of the many different critical-theoretical positions it is possible to adopt in reading texts. So:

(1) Identify four different critical theories from the twentieth century. It makes no real difference which you choose.

(2) Spend some time familiarizing yourself with each of these theories. If you wish, it is perfectly acceptable to begin with an 'introduction' text that highlights some of the key points of your chosen theories. However, at some stage in this process you will also need to return to at least one original/primary text for each of the theories you are working on. Again, it doesn't much matter which you choose, but it is essential that you engage with primary material at some point.

(3) Once you feel you have a working knowledge of each of your four theories, imagine a round-table discussion between four different people, each of whom represents one of the theories you have chosen. These four people are going to debate different topics, all the time speaking (only) from their identified theoretical positions. The topic(s) for discussion will be randomly selected by you (television, football, celebrity, space travel, etc.). The key thing is that each person remains in character (theory) throughout.

(4) Write the discussion they have between them on a chosen topic.

If carried out successfully, the outcome of this exercise will be a much greater appreciation of the way in which each of your selected theories works. In having to think only in terms of these theories, you have to consider their implications closely, which should help you as you move forward into specific textual readings. The idea is that you become a more informed and aware theoretical critic.

Suggested further reading

Aristotle, *Poetics* (c. 330 BC) – for some, the origin of literary criticism.

Eagleton, T., *Criticism and Ideology* (1978) – insightful on the relationship between criticism and the political assumptions that underpin it.

Gay, P. (ed.), *The Freud Reader* (1995) – full of essays by one of the most influential theoretical voices of recent centuries.

Horace, 'On the Art of Poetry' (c.13 BC) – another founding text of modern literary-critical studies.

Wordsworth, 'Advertisement' to the *Lyrical Ballads* (1798) – literary criticism by any other name, Wordsworth defines the essence and spirit of his version of Romanticism.

French feminism:

Cixous, H., 'The Laugh of the Medusa' (1976) – significant for (among other things) its definition of *écriture féminine*.

Irigaray, L., *The Speculum of the Other Woman* (1985 trans.) – a response to the claimed exclusion of women from philosophy and psychoanalysis.

—— *The Sex Which Is Not One* (1985 trans.) – a rejection of Lacan (who had been a key influence) and Western science more generally, for its blindness to the lives and plight of women.

Kristeva, J., *Powers of Horror* (1984 trans.) – contains a definition of 'abjection' and its role within the construction of individual identity.

—— *New Maladies of the Soul* (1995 trans.) – perhaps the clearest summation of Kristeva's views on feminism.

A selection from the many critical theory 'primers'

Culler, J., *Literary Theory: A Very Short Introduction* (2000).

Eagleton, M., (ed.) *Feminist Literary Theory: A Reader* (1995).

Eagleton, T., *Literary Theory: An Introduction* (1983).

Eagleton, T. and Drew Milne, *Marxist Literary Theory: A Reader* (1995).

Easthope, A. and Kate McGowan, *A Critical and Cultural Theory Reader* (1992).

Mongia, P., *Contemporary Postcolonial Theory: A Reader* (1996).

Rice, P. and Patricia Waugh, (eds), *Modern Literary Theory: A Reader* (1989).

Rivkin, J. and Michael Ryan (eds), *Literary Theory: An Anthology* (1997).

Stepping things up

Once you have completed all the exercises in this chapter, and feel comfortable that you have absorbed the ideas, perspectives and approaches it has discussed, you are ready to engage in some more challenging work:

(1) What differences are there between later twentieth-century critical theories and literary criticism from before that period? (Identify specific examples of each in your answer.)

(2) In what ways can pre-twentieth-century critical approaches and methods be seen as having influenced critical theories of the later twentieth century?

(3) Evaluate the strengths and weaknesses of ANY TWO critical theories. Illustrate these with specific reference to 'The Man with the Twisted Lip' (which can be found in Appendix C).

Conclusion: Unveiling the self-conscious critic

How to Read Texts began with a series of aims:

- to provide a user-friendly introduction to a range of critical approaches
- to encourage degree-level students to think about their own critical reading and its assumptions
- to test these assumptions through practical exploration
- to show the ways in which creativity and criticism can inform each other
- to give a sense of the historical development of literary criticism
- to consider the methods and assumptions of different critical approaches

Throughout it has been the intention to make this introductory book both interesting and engaging, allowing undergraduate students to develop their critical voices. The idea has been to make literary criticism something that readers participate in rather than observe from the sidelines. Which is why the chapters have been arranged in such a way as to cumulatively expand your critical skills, knowledge and self-awareness as a reader. Quite deliberately, the book began with you taking stock of your own initial thoughts and perceptions about a range of issues to do with the reading and interpretation of texts. It was an attempt to start you off on the process of becoming self-conscious about the way you read. So, in Chapter 1 you completed a questionnaire; your answers and their implications identified your perspectives and presuppositions about reading and texts. This was significant because it was the first stage in you thinking about different ways of reading other than your own. For many of you this will have been the first opportunity to really think about how you read and interpret texts.

As a conclusion to this book, you are now required to complete the critical self-awareness questionnaire again. The questions are the same, the only difference is that you should answer in light of all that you have read and learnt since you first completed the questionnaire. This is no more about establishing if you have come up with the right answers than it was the first time around, but is about completing the circle begun in that first chapter and allowing you to see whether you still think the same things as you did at the beginning or whether some of your views have changed. If change has taken place, hopefully you will have a clear sense of why and how. If not, likewise. Either way, don't feel restricted by your answers or where you end up on the line graph. It is possible, some would even say desirable, for critics to inhabit different positions at different times, and none of these positions are better or worse than any other.

The undergraduate questionnaire revisited

(1) You do not need to know anything about the historical background of a text to understand what it means: AGREE/DISAGREE/DON'T KNOW

(2) University English literature courses should include the study of texts from all over the world, possibly even those originally written in languages other than English: AGREE/DISAGREE/DON'T KNOW

(3) The meaning of the text comes through the words on the page: AGREE/DISAGREE/DON'T KNOW

(4) Some texts have a universal meaning that is relevant to all societies, both past and present: AGREE/DISAGREE/DON'T KNOW

(5) When reading a text it is important to have some familiarity with other texts in the same genre and by the same author: AGREE/DISAGREE/DON'T KNOW

(6) 'English literature' is a term that should refer to work by 'great' writers such as Shakespeare: AGREE/DISAGREE/DON'T KNOW

(7) When interpreting a text it is impossible to ignore issues such as ethnicity and gender: AGREE/DISAGREE/DON'T KNOW

(8) Genre fiction (such as romance and crime fiction) is not as well written as the classics: AGREE/DISAGREE/DON'T KNOW

(9) The critical reading of a text should focus mostly on the patterns of language and symbolism: AGREE/DISAGREE/DON'T KNOW

(10) Reading and interpreting literary texts is a critical, not a creative, activity: AGREE/DISAGREE/DON'T KNOW

Once you have given sufficient thought to each of these and noted your answers, return to the first chapter of the book and see where you end up on the line graph this time.

Thinking about ... your own development as a reader

- Which answers you have given are the same as the first time you completed the questionnaire? Do you understand why? For example, if you still disagree with the statement that textual meaning comes through the words on the page, do you disagree for the same reasons as before? Do you now feel that you have a more solid base of knowledge to make such a judgement?

- Which answers are different from the first time around? Identify why it is that you have changed your mind.

Reading as exploration

From now on, when you explore texts you will hopefully be doing so with a greater appreciation of the gamut of different critical perspectives that can be applied to texts, as well as an understanding of the strengths and weaknesses of these. You should have a greater clarity as to the nature of the relationship between author, reader and text, of the relationship between texts and identity, of universalism, of the meanings of 'literature', and a range of other issues and debates.

You should certainly have the skills and knowledge to be able to evaluate:

- creativity in criticism
- close reading
- biographical reading
- contextual reading
- theoretical reading.

And, as has hopefully become clear over the course of *How to Read Texts*, the issue is not the particular nature of your opinions in each of these critical areas. Criticism is intended to open up exploratory possibilities, not narrow down your potential to be imaginative, perceptive and creative in your reading. What *is* important, however, is that any critical position you adopt is thought through, considered, and that you are able to support your interpretations with evidence.

This is how a self-conscious critic works; when they utilize a particular method of reading they know why they are doing so and what the characteristics and benefits of that method are. This knowledge and self-awareness brings with it a critical confidence, the sort of confidence you get from knowing why you are doing something and believing that it is the most appropriate thing to be doing at any one time. Your self-awareness should also mean that when you read an interpretation of a text written by someone else you can recognize which critical perspective the critic is adopting, knowledge which can then provide the basis for your own reading of their reading. At this point, rather impressively, you will be critiquing the critics!

So, *How to Read Texts* is not about a particular doctrine or philosophy or critical perspective. Sure, within the chapters of the book certain assumptions have been made about reading and texts, but these have always been identified as exactly that, assumptions, allowing you the option of choosing to think differently. The discussion has not been about converting you to one *school* of criticism or other, or persuading you of the validity of a single critical approach.

Conclusion: Unveiling the self-conscious critic

The primary aim of this book has been to encourage you to consider criticism in all its guises and to identify which particular approach to use and in which circumstances. The idea is to give you the confidence to make critical decisions of your own and to explore texts on the basis of these decisions. Part of this is about encouraging you to experiment with different approaches, using some in tandem, reworking and challenging others. Criticism is a vast and wide-ranging field, and it is up to you to embrace the potential of this as you move forward as a creative-critical reader in your own right.

For the most effective critics are able to look across the range of voices that make up our colourful critical history and decide for themselves, based on their own knowledge and understanding, which approach suits them best at any given time (or in relation to any given text). Therein they accommodate other critical 'voices' into their own as they develop a more confident critical perspective for themselves. This allows the possibility of inhabiting different critical territories at different times, being imaginative and inventive, and refusing to slavishly adopt the perspectives of others. Self-conscious reader-critics instead have the confidence to mark out their own ground. Their criticism can be *truly* creative in the best senses of the word. And, no matter how intimidating the process of exploring the rich variety of texts might seem at times, especially for those only just setting out on the road to becoming accomplished readers, eventually, I hope, this will (quite rightly) be seen as a glorious opportunity to be grasped with both hands.

Appendix A

'The Tell-Tale Heart'
by Edgar Allan Poe
(1843)

TRUE! – nervous – very, very dreadfully nervous I had been and am; but why *will* you say that I am mad? The disease had sharpened my senses – not destroyed – not dulled them. Above all was the sense of hearing acute. I heard all things in the heaven and in the earth. I heard many things in hell. How, then, am I mad? Hearken! and observe how healthily – how calmly I can tell you the whole story.

It is impossible to say how first the idea entered my brain; but once conceived, it haunted me day and night. Object there was none. Passion there was none. I loved the old man. He had never wronged me. He had never given me insult. For his gold I had no desire. I think it was his eye! yes, it was this! He had the eye of a vulture – a pale blue eye, with a film over it. Whenever it fell upon me, my blood ran cold; and so by degrees – very gradually – I made up my mind to take the life of the old man, and thus rid myself of the eye forever.

Now this is the point. You fancy me mad. Madmen know nothing. But you should have seen me. You should have seen how wisely I proceeded – with what caution – with what foresight – with what dissimulation I went to work! I was never kinder to the old man than during the whole week before I killed him. And every night, about midnight, I turned the latch of his door and opened it – oh so gently! And then, when I had made an opening sufficient for my head, I put in a dark lantern, all closed, closed, that no light shone out, and then I thrust in my head. Oh, you would have laughed to see how cunningly I thrust it in! I moved it slowly – very, very slowly, so that I might not disturb the old man's sleep. It took me an hour to place my whole head within the opening so far that I could see him as he lay upon his bed. Ha! would a madman have been so wise as this? And then, when my head was well in the room, I undid the lantern cautiously – oh, so cautiously – cautiously (for the hinges creaked) – I undid it just so much that a single thin ray fell upon the vulture eye. And this I did for seven long nights – every night just at midnight – but I found the eye always closed; and so it was impossible to do the work; for it was not the old man who vexed me, but his Evil Eye. And every morning, when the day broke, I went boldly into the chamber, and spoke courageously to him, calling him by name in a hearty tone, and inquiring how he has passed the night. So you see he would have been a very profound old man, indeed, to suspect that every night, just at twelve, I looked in upon him while he slept.

Upon the eighth night I was more than usually cautious in opening the door. A watch's minute hand moves more quickly than did mine. Never before that night had I felt the extent of my own powers – of my sagacity. I could scarcely contain my feelings of triumph. To think that there I was, opening the door, little by little, and he not even to dream of my secret deeds or thoughts. I fairly chuckled at the idea; and perhaps he heard me; for he moved on the bed suddenly, as if startled. Now you may think that I drew back – but no. His room was as black as pitch with the thick darkness (for the shutters were close fastened, through fear of robbers), and so I knew that he could not see the opening of the door, and I kept pushing it on steadily, steadily.

I had my head in, and was about to open the lantern, when my thumb slipped upon the tin fastening, and the old man sprang up in bed, crying out – 'Who's there?'

I kept quite still and said nothing. For a whole hour I did not move a muscle, and in the meantime I did not hear him lie down. He was still sitting up in the bed listening; – just as I have done, night after night, hearkening to the death watches in the wall.

Presently I heard a slight groan, and I knew it was the groan of mortal terror. It was not a groan of pain or of grief – oh, no! – it was the low stifled sound that arises from the bottom of the soul when overcharged with awe. I knew the sound well. Many a night, just at midnight, when all the world slept, it has welled up from my own bosom, deepening, with its dreadful echo, the terrors that distracted me. I say I knew it well. I knew what the old man felt, and pitied him, although I chuckled at heart. I knew that he had been lying awake ever since the first slight noise, when he had turned in the bed. His fears had been ever since growing upon him. He had been trying to fancy them causeless, but could not. He had been saying to himself – 'It is nothing but the wind in the chimney – it is only a mouse crossing the floor', or 'It is merely a cricket which has made a single chirp.' Yes, he had been trying to comfort himself with these suppositions: but he had found all in vain. All in vain; because Death, in approaching him had stalked with his black shadow before him, and enveloped the victim. And it was the mournful influence of the unperceived shadow that caused him to feel – although he neither saw nor heard – to feel the presence of my head within the room.

When I had waited a long time, very patiently, without hearing him lie down, I resolved to open a little – a very, very little crevice in the lantern. So I opened it – you cannot imagine how stealthily, stealthily – until, at length a simple dim ray, like the thread of the spider, shot from out the crevice and fell full upon the vulture eye.

It was open – wide, wide open – and I grew furious as I gazed upon it. I saw it with perfect distinctness – all a dull blue, with a hideous veil over it that chilled the very marrow in my bones; but I could see nothing else of the old man's face or person: for I had directed the ray as if by instinct, precisely upon the damned spot.

And have I not told you that what you mistake for madness is but over-acuteness of the sense? – now, I say, there came to my ears a low, dull, quick sound, such as a watch makes when enveloped in cotton. I knew that sound well, too. It was the beating of the old man's heart. It increased my fury, as the beating of a drum stimulates the soldier into courage.

But even yet I refrained and kept still. I scarcely breathed. I held the lantern motionless. I tried how steadily I could maintain the ray upon the eye. Meantime the hellish tattoo of the heart increased. It grew quicker and quicker, and louder and louder every instant. The old man's terror must have been extreme! It grew louder, I say, louder every moment! – do you mark me well I have told you that I am nervous: so I am. And now at the dead hour of the night, amid the dreadful silence of that old house, so strange a noise as this excited me to uncontrollable terror. Yet, for some minutes longer I refrained and stood still. But the beating grew louder, louder! I thought the heart must burst. And now a new anxiety seized me – the sound would be heard by a neighbour! The old man's hour had come! With a loud yell, I threw open the lantern and leaped into the room. He shrieked once – once only. In an instant I dragged him to the floor, and pulled the heavy bed over him. I then smiled gaily, to find the deed so far done. But, for many minutes, the heart beat on with a muffled sound. This, however, did not vex me; it would not be heard through the wall. At length it ceased. The old man was dead. I removed the bed and examined the corpse. Yes, he was stone, stone dead. I placed my hand upon the heart and held it there many minutes. There was no pulsation. He was stone dead. His eye would trouble me no more.

If still you think me mad, you will think so no longer when I describe the wise precautions I took for the concealment of the body. The night waned, and I worked hastily, but in silence. First of all I dismembered the corpse. I cut off the head and the arms and the legs.

I then took up three planks from the flooring of the chamber, and deposited all between the scantlings. I then replaced the boards so cleverly, so cunningly, that no human eye – not even his – could have detected any thing wrong. There was nothing to wash out – no stain of any kind – no blood-spot whatever. I had been too wary for that. A tub had caught all – ha! ha!

When I had made an end of these labors, it was four o'clock – still dark as midnight. As the bell sounded the hour, there came a knocking at the street door. I went down to open it with a light heart, – for what had I now to fear? There entered three men, who introduced themselves, with perfect suavity, as officers of the police. A shriek had been heard by a neighbour during the night; suspicion of foul play had been aroused; information had been lodged at the police office, and they (the officers) had been deputed to search the premises.

I smiled, – for what had I to fear? I bade the gentlemen welcome. The shriek, I said, was my own in a dream. The old man, I mentioned, was absent in the country. I took my visitors all over the house. I bade them search – search well. I led them, at length, to his chamber. I showed them his treasures, secure, undisturbed. In the enthusiasm of my confidence, I brought chairs into the room, and desired them here to rest from their fatigues, while I myself, in the wild audacity of my perfect triumph, placed my own seat upon the very spot beneath which reposed the corpse of the victim.

The officers were satisfied. My manner had convinced them. I was singularly at ease. They sat, and while I answered cheerily, they chatted of familiar things. But, ere long, I felt myself getting pale and wished them gone. My head ached, and I fancied a ringing in my ears: but still they sat and still chatted. The ringing became more distinct: – It continued and became more distinct: I talked more freely to get rid of the feeling: but it continued and gained definiteness – until, at length, I found that the noise was not within my ears.

No doubt I now grew very pale; – but I talked more fluently, and with a heightened voice. Yet the sound increased – and what could I do? It was a low, dull, quick sound – much such a sound as a watch makes when enveloped in cotton. I gasped for breath – and yet the officers heard it not. I talked more quickly – more vehemently; but the noise steadily increased. I arose and argued about trifles, in a high key and with violent gesticulations; but the noise steadily increased. Why would they not be gone? I paced the floor to and fro with heavy strides, as if excited to fury by the observations of the men – but the noise steadily increased. Oh God! what could I do? I foamed – I raved – I swore! I swung the chair upon which I had been sitting, and grated it upon the boards, but the noise arose over all and continually increased. It grew louder – louder – louder! And still the men chatted pleasantly, and smiled. Was it possible they heard not? Almighty God! – no, no! They heard! – they suspected! – they knew! – they were making a mockery of my horror! – this I thought, and this I think. But anything was better than this agony! Anything was more tolerable than this derision! I could bear those hypocritical smiles no longer! I felt that I must scream or die! and now – again! – hark! louder! louder! louder! louder!

'Villains!' I shrieked, 'dissemble no more! I admit the deed! – tear up the planks! here, here! – It is the beating of his hideous heart!'

— THE END —

Appendix B

'The Tyger'
by William Blake
(1794)

Tyger! Tyger! burning bright
In the forests of the night,
What immortal hand or eye
Could frame thy fearful symmetry?

In what distant deeps or skies
Burnt the fire of thine eyes?
On what wings dare he aspire?
What the hand dare sieze the fire?

And what shoulder, and what art.
Could twist the sinews of thy heart?
And when thy heart began to beat,
What dread hand? and what dread feet?

What the hammer? what the chain?
In what furnace was thy brain?
What the anvil? what dread grasp
Dare its deadly terrors clasp?

When the stars threw down their spears,
And watered heaven with their tears,
Did he smile his work to see?
Did he who made the Lamb make thee?

Tyger! Tyger! burning bright
In the forests of the night,
What immortal hand or eye
Dare frame thy fearful symmetry?

1794

Appendix C

'The Man with the Twisted Lip'
by Arthur Conan Doyle
(1891)

Isa Whitney, brother of the late Elias Whitney, D D., Principal of the Theological College of St George's, was much addicted to opium. The habit grew upon him, as I understand, from some foolish freak when he was at college; for having read De Quincey's description of his dreams and sensations, he had drenched his tobacco with laudanum in an attempt to produce the same effects. He found, as so many more have done, that the practice is easier to attain than to get rid of, and for many years he continued to be a slave to the drug, an object of mingled horror and pity to his friends and relatives. I can see him now, with yellow, pasty face, drooping lids, and pin-point pupils, all huddled in a chair, the wreck and ruin of a noble man.

One night – it was in June, '89 – there came a ring to my bell, about the hour when a man gives his first yawn and glances at the clock. I sat up in my chair, and my wife laid her needle-work down in her lap and made a little face of disappointment.

'A patient!' said she. 'You'll have to go out.'

I groaned, for I was newly come back from a weary day.

We heard the door open, a few hurried words, and then quick steps upon the linoleum. Our own door flew open, and a lady, clad in some dark-coloured stuff, with a black veil, entered the room.

'You will excuse my calling so late,' she began, and then, suddenly losing her self-control, she ran forward, threw her arms about my wife's neck, and sobbed upon her shoulder. 'Oh, I'm in such trouble!' she cried; 'I do so want a little help.'

'Why,' said my wife, pulling up her veil, 'it is Kate Whitney. How you startled me, Kate! I had not an idea who you were when you came in.'

'I didn't know what to do, so I came straight to you.' That was always the way. Folk who were in grief came to my wife like birds to a lighthouse.

'It was very sweet of you to come. Now, you must have some wine and water, and sit here comfortably and tell us all about it. Or should you rather that I sent James off to bed?'

'Oh, no, no! I want the doctor's advice and help, too. It's about Isa. He has not been home for two days. I am so frightened about him!'

It was not the first time that she had spoken to us of her husband's trouble, to me as a doctor, to my wife as an old friend and school companion. We soothed and comforted her by such words as we could find. Did she know where her husband was? Was it possible that we could bring him back to her?

It seems that it was. She had the surest information that of late he had, when the fit was on him, made use of an opium den in the farthest east of the City. Hitherto his orgies had always been confined to one day, and he had come back, twitching and shattered, in the evening. But now the spell had been upon him eight-and-forty hours, and he lay there, doubtless among the dregs of the docks, breathing in the poison or sleeping off the effects. There he was to be found, she was sure of it, at the Bar of Gold, in Upper Swandam Lane. But what was she to do? How could she, a young and timid woman, make her way into such a place and pluck her husband out from among the ruffians who surrounded him?

There was the case, and of course there was but one way out of it. Might I not escort her to this place? And then, as a second thought, why should she come at all? I was Isa Whitney's medical adviser, and as such I had influence over him. I could manage it better if I were alone. I promised her on my word that I would send him home in a cab within two hours if he were indeed at the address which she had given me. And so in ten minutes I had left my armchair and cheery sitting-room behind me, and was speeding eastward in a hansom on a strange errand, as it seemed to me at the time, though the future only could show how strange it was to be.

But there was no great difficulty in the first stage of my adventure. Upper Swandam Lane is a vile alley lurking behind the high wharves which line the north side of the river to the east of London Bridge. Between a slop-shop and a gin-shop, approached by a steep flight of steps leading down to a black gap like the mouth of a cave, I found the den of which I was in search. Ordering my cab to wait, I passed down the steps, worn hollow in the centre by the ceaseless tread of drunken feet; and by the light of a flickering oil-lamp above the door I found the latch and made my way into a long, low room, thick and heavy with the brown opium smoke, and terraced with wooden berths, like the forecastle of an emigrant ship.

Through the gloom one could dimly catch a glimpse of bodies lying in strange fantastic poses, bowed shoulders, bent knees, heads thrown back, and chins pointing upward, with here and there a dark, lack-lustre eye turned upon the newcomer. Out of the black shadows there glimmered little red circles of light, now bright, now faint, as the burning poison waxed or waned in the bowls of the metal pipes. The most lay silent, but some muttered to themselves, and others talked together in a strange, low, monotonous voice, their conversation coming in gushes, and then suddenly tailing off into silence, each mumbling out his own thoughts and paying little heed to the words of his neighbour. At the farther end was a small brazier of burning charcoal, beside which on a three-legged wooden stool there sat a tall, thin old man, with his jaw resting upon his two fists, and his elbows upon his knees, staring into the fire.

As I entered, a sallow Malay attendant had hurried up with a pipe for me and a supply of the drug, beckoning me to an empty berth.

'Thank you. I have not come to stay,' said I. 'There is a friend of mine here, Mr Isa Whitney, and I wish to speak with him.'

There was a movement and an exclamation from my right, and peering through the gloom I saw Whitney, pale, haggard, and unkempt, staring out at me.

'My God! It's Watson,' said he. He was in a pitiable state of reaction, with every nerve in a twitter. 'I say, Watson, what o'clock is it?'

'Nearly eleven.'

'Of what day?'

'Of Friday, June 19th.'

'Good heavens! I thought it was Wednesday. It is Wednesday. What d'you want to frighten the chap for?' He sank his face onto his arms and began to sob in a high treble key.

'I tell you that it is Friday, man. Your wife has been waiting this two days for you. You should be ashamed of yourself!'

'So I am. But you've got mixed, Watson, for I have only been here a few hours, three pipes, four pipes – I forget how many. But I'll go home with you. I wouldn't frighten Kate – poor little Kate. Give me your hand! Have you a cab?'

'Yes, I have one waiting.'

'Then I shall go in it. But I must owe something. Find what I owe, Watson. I am all off colour. I can do nothing for myself.'

I walked down the narrow passage between the double row of sleepers, holding my breath to keep out the vile, stupefying fumes of the drug, and looking about for the manager. As I passed the tall man who sat by the brazier I felt a sudden pluck at my skirt, and a low voice whispered, 'Walk past me, and then look back at me.' The words fell quite distinctly upon my ear. I glanced down. They could only have come from the old man at my side, and yet he sat now as absorbed as ever, very thin, very wrinkled, bent with age, an opium pipe dangling down from between his knees, as though it had dropped in sheer lassitude from his fingers.

I took two steps forward and looked back. It took all my self-control to prevent me from breaking out into a cry of astonishment. He had turned his back so that none could see him but I. His form had filled out, his wrinkles were gone, the dull eyes had regained their fire, and there, sitting by the fire and grinning at my surprise, was none other than Sherlock Holmes. He made a slight motion to me to approach him, and instantly, as he turned his face half round to the company once more, subsided into a doddering, loose-lipped senility.

'Holmes!' I whispered, 'what on earth are you doing in this den?'

'As low as you can,' he answered; 'I have excellent ears. If you would have the great kindness to get rid of that sottish friend of yours I should be exceedingly glad to have a little talk with you.'

'I have a cab outside.'

'Then pray send him home in it. You may safely trust him, for he appears to be too limp to get into any mischief. I should recommend you also to send a note by the cabman to your wife to say that you have thrown in your lot with me. If you will wait outside, I shall be with you in five minutes.'

It was difficult to refuse any of Sherlock Holmes's requests, for they were always so exceedingly definite, and put forward with such a quiet air of mastery. I felt, however, that when Whitney was once confined in the cab my mission was practically accomplished; and for the rest, I could not wish anything better than to be associated with my friend in one of those singular adventures which were the normal condition of his existence. In a few minutes I had written my note, paid Whitney's bill, led him out to the cab, and seen him driven through the darkness. In a very short time a decrepit figure had emerged from the opium den, and I was walking down the street with Sherlock Holmes. For two streets he shuffled along with a bent back and an uncertain foot. Then, glancing quickly round, he straightened himself out and burst into a hearty fit of laughter.

'I suppose, Watson,' said he, 'that you imagine that I have added opium-smoking to cocaine injections, and all the other little weaknesses on which you have favoured me with your medical views.'

'I was certainly surprised to find you there.'

'But not more so than I to find you.'

'I came to find a friend.'

'And I to find an enemy.'

'An enemy?'

'Yes; one of my natural enemies, or, shall I say, my natural prey. Briefly, Watson, I am in the midst of a very remarkable inquiry, and I have hoped to find a clew in the incoherent ramblings of these sots, as I have done before now. Had I been recognised in that den my life would not have been worth an hour's purchase; for I have used it before now for my own purposes, and the rascally Lascar who runs it has sworn to have vengeance upon me. There is a trap-door at the back of that building, near the corner of Paul's Wharf, which could tell some strange tales of what has passed through it upon the moonless nights.'

'What! You do not mean bodies?'

'Ay, bodies, Watson. We should be rich men if we had 1000 pounds for every poor devil who has been done to death in that den. It is the vilest murder-trap on the whole riverside, and I fear that Neville St Clair has entered it never to leave it more. But our trap should be here.' He put his two forefingers between his teeth and whistled shrilly – a signal which was answered by a similar whistle from the distance, followed shortly by the rattle of wheels and the clink of horses' hoofs.

'Now, Watson,' said Holmes, as a tall dog-cart dashed up through the gloom, throwing out two golden tunnels of yellow light from its side lanterns. 'You'll come with me, won't you?'

'If I can be of use.'

'Oh, a trusty comrade is always of use; and a chronicler still more so. My room at The Cedars is a double-bedded one.'

'The Cedars?'

'Yes; that is Mr St Clair's house. I am staying there while I conduct the inquiry.'

'Where is it, then?'

'Near Lee, in Kent. We have a seven-mile drive before us.'

'But I am all in the dark.'

'Of course you are. You'll know all about it presently. Jump up here. All right, John; we shall not need you. Here's half a crown. Look out for me to-morrow, about eleven. Give her her head. So long, then!'

He flicked the horse with his whip, and we dashed away through the endless succession of sombre and deserted streets, which widened gradually, until we were flying across a broad balustraded bridge, with the murky river flowing sluggishly beneath us. Beyond lay another dull wilderness of bricks and mortar, its silence broken only by the heavy, regular footfall of the policeman, or the songs and shouts of some belated party of revellers. A dull wrack was drifting slowly across the sky, and a star or two twinkled dimly here and there through the rifts of the clouds. Holmes drove in silence, with his head sunk upon his breast, and the air of a man who is lost in thought, while I sat beside him, curious to learn what this new quest might be which seemed to tax his powers so sorely, and yet afraid to break in upon the current of his thoughts. We had driven several miles, and were beginning to get to the fringe of the belt of suburban villas, when he shook himself, shrugged his shoulders, and lit up his pipe with the air of a man who has satisfied himself that he is acting for the best.

'You have a grand gift of silence, Watson,' said he. 'It makes you quite invaluable as a companion. Upon my word, it is a great thing for me to have someone to talk to, for my own thoughts are not over-pleasant. I was wondering what I should say to this dear little woman tonight when she meets me at the door.'

'You forget that I know nothing about it.'

'I shall just have time to tell you the facts of the case before we get to Lee. It seems absurdly simple, and yet, somehow I can get nothing to go upon. There's plenty of thread, no doubt, but I can't get the end of it into my hand. Now, I'll state the case clearly and concisely to you, Watson, and maybe you can see a spark where all is dark to me.'

'Proceed, then.'

'Some years ago – to be definite, in May, 1884 – there came to Lee a gentleman, Neville St Clair by name, who appeared to have plenty of money. He took a large villa, laid out the grounds very nicely, and lived generally in good style. By degrees he made friends in the neighbourhood, and in 1887 he married the daughter of a local brewer, by whom he now has two children. He had no occupation, but was interested in several companies and went into town as a rule in the morning, returning by the 5:14 from Cannon Street every night. Mr St Clair is now thirty-seven years of age, is a man of temperate habits, a good husband, a very affectionate father, and a man who is popular with all who know him. I may add that his whole debts at the present moment, as far as we have been able to ascertain amount to 88 pounds 10s., while he has 220 pounds standing to his credit in the Capital and Counties Bank. There is no reason, therefore, to think that money troubles have been weighing upon his mind.

'Anyway, last Monday Mr Neville St Clair went into town rather earlier than usual, remarking before he started that he had two important commissions to perform, and that he would bring his little boy home a box of bricks. Now, by the merest chance, his wife received a telegram upon this same Monday, very shortly after his departure, to the effect that a small parcel of considerable value which she had been expecting was waiting for her at the offices of the Aberdeen Shipping Company. Now, if you are well up in your London, you will know that the office of the company is in Fresno Street, which branches out of Upper Swandam Lane, where you found me tonight. Mrs St Clair had her lunch, started for the City, did some shopping, proceeded to the company's office, got her packet, and found herself at exactly 4:35 walking through Swandam Lane on her way back to the station. Have you followed me so far?'

'It is very clear.'

'If you remember, Monday was an exceedingly hot day, and Mrs St Clair walked slowly, glancing about in the hope of seeing a cab, as she did not like the neighbourhood in which she found herself. While she was walking in this way down Swandam Lane, she suddenly heard an ejaculation or cry, and was struck cold to see her husband looking down at her and, as it seemed to her, beckoning to her from a second-floor window. The window was open, and she distinctly saw his face, which she describes as being terribly agitated. He waved his hands frantically to her, and then vanished from the window so suddenly that it seemed to her that he had been plucked back by some irresistible force from behind. One singular point which struck her quick feminine eye was that although he wore some dark coat, such as he had started to town in, he had on neither collar nor necktie.

'Convinced that something was amiss with him, she rushed down the steps – for the house was none other than the opium den in which you found me to-night – and running through the front room she attempted to ascend the stairs which led to the first floor. At the foot of the stairs, however, she met this Lascar scoundrel of whom I have spoken, who thrust her back and, aided by a Dane, who acts as assistant there, pushed her out into the street. Filled with the most maddening doubts and fears, she rushed down the lane and, by rare good-fortune, met in Fresno Street a number of Constables with an Inspector, all on their way to their beat. The Inspector and two men accompanied her back, and in spite of the continued resistance of the proprietor, they made their way to the room in which Mr St Clair had last been seen. There was no sign of him there. In fact, in the whole of that floor there was no one to be found save a crippled wretch of hideous aspect, who, it seems, made his home there. Both he and the Lascar stoutly swore that no one else had been in the front room during the afternoon. So determined was their denial that the Inspector was staggered, and had almost come to believe that Mrs St Clair had been deluded when, with a cry, she sprang at a small deal box which lay upon the table and tore the lid from it. Out fell a cascade of children's bricks. It was the toy which he had promised to bring home.

'This discovery, and the evident confusion which the cripple showed, made the Inspector realise that the matter was serious. The rooms were carefully examined, and results all pointed to an abominable crime. The front room was plainly furnished as a sitting-room and led into a small bedroom, which looked out upon the back of one of the wharves. Between the wharf and the bedroom window is a narrow strip, which is dry at low tide but is covered at high tide with at least four and a half feet of water. The bedroom window was a broad one and opened from below. On examination traces of blood were to be seen upon the windowsill, and several scattered drops were visible upon the wooden floor of the bedroom. Thrust away behind a curtain in the front room were all the clothes of Mr Neville St Clair, with the exception of his coat. His boots, his socks, his hat, and his watch – all were there. There were no signs of violence upon any of these garments, and there were no other traces of Mr Neville St Clair. Out of the window he must apparently have gone for no other exit could be discovered, and the ominous bloodstains upon the sill gave little promise that he could save himself by swimming, for the tide was at its very highest at the moment of the tragedy.

'And now as to the villains who seemed to be immediately implicated in the matter. The Lascar was known to be a man of the vilest antecedents, but as, by Mrs St Clair's story, he was known to have been at the foot of the stair within a very few seconds of her husband's appearance at the window, he could hardly have been more than an accessory to the crime. His defence was one of absolute ignorance, and he protested that he had no knowledge as to the doings of Hugh Boone, his lodger, and that he could not account in any way for the presence of the missing gentleman's clothes.

'So much for the Lascar manager. Now for the sinister cripple who lives upon the second floor of the opium den, and who was certainly the last human being whose eyes rested upon Neville St Clair. His name is Hugh Boone, and his hideous face is one which is familiar to every man who goes much to the City. He is a professional beggar, though in order to avoid the police regulations he pretends to a small trade in wax vestas. Some little distance down Threadneedle Street, upon the left-hand side, there is, as you may have remarked, a small angle in the wall. Here it is that this creature takes his daily seat, cross-legged with his tiny stock of matches on his lap, and as he is a piteous spectacle a small rain of charity descends into the greasy leather cap which lies upon the pavement beside him. I have watched the fellow more than once before ever I thought of making his professional acquaintance, and I have been surprised at the harvest which he has reaped in a short time. His appearance, you see, is so remarkable that no one can pass him without observing him. A shock of orange hair, a pale face disfigured by a horrible scar, which, by its contraction, has turned up the outer edge of his upper lip, a bulldog chin, and a pair of very penetrating dark eyes, which present a singular contrast to the colour of his hair, all mark him out from amid the common crowd of mendicants and so, too, does his wit, for he is ever ready with a reply to any piece of chaff which may be thrown at him by the passers-by. This is the man whom we now learn to have been the lodger at the opium den, and to have been the last man to see the gentleman of whom we are in quest.'

'But a cripple!' said I. 'What could he have done single-handed against a man in the prime of life?'

'He is a cripple in the sense that he walks with a limp; but in other respects he appears to be a powerful and well-nurtured man. Surely your medical experience would tell you, Watson, that weakness in one limb is often compensated for by exceptional strength in the others.'

'Pray continue your narrative.'

'Mrs St Clair had fainted at the sight of the blood upon the window, and she was escorted home in a cab by the police, as her presence could be of no help to them in their investigations. Inspector Barton, who had charge of the case, made a very careful examination of the premises, but without finding anything which threw any light upon the matter. One mistake had been made in not arresting Boone instantly, as he was allowed some few minutes during which he might have communicated with his friend the Lascar, but this fault was soon remedied, and he was seized and searched, without anything being found which could incriminate him. There were, it is true, some blood-stains upon his right shirt-sleeve, but he pointed to his ring-finger, which had been cut near the nail, and explained that the bleeding came from there, adding that he had been to the window not long before, and that the stains which had been observed there came doubtless from the same source. He denied strenuously having ever seen Mr Neville St Clair and swore that the presence of the clothes in his room was as much a mystery to him as to the police. As to Mrs St Clair's assertion that she had actually seen her husband at the window, he declared that she must have been either mad or dreaming. He was removed, loudly protesting, to the police-station, while the Inspector remained upon the premises in the hope that the ebbing tide might afford some fresh clue.

'And it did, though they hardly found upon the mud-bank what they had feared to find. It was Neville St Clair's coat, and not Neville St Clair, which lay uncovered as the tide receded. And what do you think they found in the pockets?'

'I cannot imagine.'

'No, I don't think you would guess. Every pocket stuffed with pennies and half-pennies – 421 pennies and 270 half-pennies. It was no wonder that it had not been swept away by the tide. But a human body is a different matter. There is a fierce eddy between the wharf and the house. It seemed likely enough that the weighted coat had remained when the stripped body had been sucked away into the river.'

'But I understand that all the other clothes were found in the room. Would the body be dressed in a coat alone?'

'No, sir, but the facts might be met speciously enough. Suppose that this man Boone had thrust Neville St Clair through the window, there is no human eye which could have seen the deed. What would he do then? It would of course instantly strike him that he must get rid of the tell-tale garments. He would seize the coat, then, and be in the act of throwing it out, when it would occur to him that it would swim and not sink. He has little time, for he has heard the scuffle downstairs when the wife tried to force her way up, and perhaps he has already heard from his Lascar confederate that the police are hurrying up the street. There is not an instant to be lost. He rushes to some secret hoard, where he has accumulated the fruits of his beggary, and he stuffs all the coins upon which he can lay his hands into the pockets to make sure of the coat's sinking. He throws it out, and would have done the same with the other garments had not he heard the rush of steps below, and only just had time to close the window when the police appeared.'

'It certainly sounds feasible.'

'Well, we will take it as a working hypothesis for want of a better one. Boone, as I have told you, was arrested and taken to the station, but it could not be shown that there had ever before been anything against him. He had for years been known as a professional beggar, but his life appeared to have been a very quiet and innocent one. There the matter stands at present, and the questions which have to be solved – what Neville St Clair was doing in the opium den, what happened to him when there, where is he now, and what Hugh Boone had to do with his disappearance – are all as far from a solution as ever. I confess that I cannot recall any case within my experience which looked at the first glance so simple and yet which presented such difficulties.'

While Sherlock Holmes had been detailing this singular series of events, we had been whirling through the outskirts of the great town until the last straggling houses had been left behind, and we rattled along with a country hedge upon either side of us. Just as he finished, however, we drove through two scattered villages, where a few lights still glimmered in the windows.

'We are on the outskirts of Lee,' said my companion. 'We have touched on three English counties in our short drive, starting in Middlesex, passing over an angle of Surrey, and ending in Kent. See that light among the trees? That is The Cedars, and beside that lamp sits a woman whose anxious ears have already, I have little doubt, caught the clink of our horse's feet.'

'But why are you not conducting the case from Baker Street?' I asked.

'Because there are many inquiries which must be made out here. Mrs St Clair has most kindly put two rooms at my disposal, and you may rest assured that she will have nothing but a welcome for my friend and colleague. I hate to meet her, Watson, when I have no news of her husband. Here we are. Whoa, there, whoa!'

We had pulled up in front of a large villa which stood within its own grounds. A stable-boy had run out to the horse's head, and springing down, I followed Holmes up the small, winding gravel-drive which led to the house. As we approached, the door flew open, and a little blonde woman stood in the opening, clad in some sort of light mousseline de soie, with a touch of fluffy pink chiffon at her neck and wrists. She stood with her figure outlined against the flood of light, one hand upon the door, one half-raised in her eagerness, her body slightly bent, her head and face protruded, with eager eyes and parted lips, a standing question.

'Well?' she cried, 'well?' And then, seeing that there were two of us, she gave a cry of hope which sank into a groan as she saw that my companion shook his head and shrugged his shoulders.

'No good news?'

'None.'

'No bad?'

'No.'

'Thank God for that. But come in. You must be weary, for you have had a long day.'

'This is my friend, Dr Watson. He has been of most vital use to me in several of my cases, and a lucky chance has made it possible for me to bring him out and associate him with this investigation.'

'I am delighted to see you,' said she, pressing my hand warmly. 'You will, I am sure, forgive anything that may be wanting in our arrangements, when you consider the blow which has come so suddenly upon us.'

'My dear madam,' said I, 'I am an old campaigner, and if I were not I can very well see that no apology is needed. If I can be of any assistance, either to you or to my friend here, I shall be indeed happy.'

'Now, Mr. Sherlock Holmes,' said the lady as we entered a well-lit dining-room, upon the table of which a cold supper had been laid out, 'I should very much like to ask you one or two plain questions, to which I beg that you will give a plain answer.'

'Certainly, madam.'

'Do not trouble about my feelings. I am not hysterical, nor given to fainting. I simply wish to hear your real, real opinion.'

'Upon what point?'

'In your heart of hearts, do you think that Neville is alive?'

Sherlock Holmes seemed to be embarrassed by the question. 'Frankly, now!' she repeated, standing upon the rug and looking keenly down at him as he leaned back in a basket-chair.

'Frankly, then, madam, I do not.'

'You think that he is dead?'

'I do.'

'Murdered?'

'I don't say that. Perhaps.'

'And on what day did he meet his death?'

'On Monday.'

'Then perhaps, Mr Holmes, you will be good enough to explain how it is that I have received a letter from him today.'

Sherlock Holmes sprang out of his chair as if he had been galvanised.

'What!' he roared.

'Yes, today.' She stood smiling, holding up a little slip of paper in the air.

'May I see it?'

'Certainly.'

He snatched it from her in his eagerness, and smoothing it out upon the table he drew over the lamp and examined it intently. I had left my chair and was gazing at it over his shoulder. The envelope was a very coarse one and was stamped with the Gravesend postmark and with the date of that very day, or rather of the day before, for it was considerably after midnight.

'Coarse writing,' murmured Holmes. 'Surely this is not your husband's writing, madam?'

'No, but the enclosure is.'

'I perceive also that whoever addressed the envelope had to go and inquire as to the address.'

'How can you tell that?'

'The name, you see, is in perfectly black ink, which has dried itself. The rest is of the greyish colour, which shows that blotting-paper has been used. If it had been written straight off, and then blotted, none would be of a deep black shade. This man has written the name, and there has then been a pause before he wrote the address, which can only mean that he was not familiar with it. It is, of course, a trifle, but there is nothing so important as trifles. Let us now see the letter. Ha! there has been an enclosure here!'

'Yes, there was a ring. His signet-ring.'

'And you are sure that this is your husband's hand?'

'One of his hands.'

'One?'

'His hand when he wrote hurriedly. It is very unlike his usual writing, and yet I know it well.'

' "Dearest do not be frightened. All will come well. There is a huge error which it may take some little time to rectify. Wait in patience. NEVILLE." Written in pencil upon the fly-leaf of a book, octavo size, no water-mark. Hum! Posted to-day in Gravesend by a man with a dirty thumb. Ha! And the flap has been gummed, if I am not very much in error, by a person who had been chewing tobacco. And you have no doubt that it is your husband's hand, madam?'

'None. Neville wrote those words.'

'And they were posted today at Gravesend. Well, Mrs St Clair, the clouds lighten, though I should not venture to say that the danger is over.'

'But he must be alive, Mr Holmes.'

'Unless this is a clever forgery to put us on the wrong scent. The ring, after all, proves nothing. It may have been taken from him.'

'No, no; it is, it is his very own writing!'

'Very well. It may, however, have been written on Monday and only posted today.'

'That is possible.'

'If so, much may have happened between.'

'Oh, you must not discourage me, Mr Holmes. I know that all is well with him. There is so keen a sympathy between us that I should know if evil came upon him. On the very day that I saw him last he cut himself in the bedroom, and yet I in the dining-room rushed upstairs instantly with the utmost certainty that something had happened. Do you think that I would respond to such a trifle and yet be ignorant of his death?'

'I have seen too much not to know that the impression of a woman may be more valuable than the conclusion of an analytical reasoner. And in this letter you certainly have a very strong piece of evidence to corroborate your view. But if your husband is alive and able to write letters, why should he remain away from you?'

'I cannot imagine. It is unthinkable.'

'And on Monday he made no remarks before leaving you?'

'No.'

'And you were surprised to see him in Swandam Lane?'

'Very much so.'

'Was the window open?'

'Yes.'

'Then he might have called to you?'

'He might.'

'He only, as I understand, gave an inarticulate cry?'

'Yes.'

'A call for help, you thought?'

'Yes. He waved his hands.'

'But it might have been a cry of surprise. Astonishment at the unexpected sight of you might cause him to throw up his hands?'

'It is possible.'

'And you thought he was pulled back?'

'He disappeared so suddenly.'

'He might have leaped back. You did not see anyone else in the room?'

'No, but this horrible man confessed to having been there, and the Lascar was at the foot of the stairs.'

'Quite so. Your husband, as far as you could see, had his ordinary clothes on?'

'But without his collar or tie. I distinctly saw his bare throat.'

'Had he ever spoken of Swandam Lane?'

'Never.'

'Had he ever showed any signs of having taken opium?'

'Never.'

'Thank you, Mrs St Clair. Those are the principal points about which I wished to be absolutely clear. We shall now have a little supper and then retire, for we may have a very busy day tomorrow.'

A large and comfortable double-bedded room had been placed at our disposal, and I was quickly between the sheets, for I was weary after my night of adventure. Sherlock Holmes was a man, however, who, when he had an unsolved problem upon his mind, would go for days, and even for a week, without rest, turning it over, rearranging his facts, looking at it from every point of view until he had either fathomed it or convinced himself that his data were insufficient. It was soon evident to me that he was now preparing for an all-night sitting. He took off his coat and waistcoat, put on a large blue dressing-gown, and then wandered about the room collecting pillows from his bed and cushions from the sofa and armchairs. With these he constructed a sort of Eastern divan, upon which he perched himself cross-legged, with an ounce of shag tobacco and a box of matches laid out in front of him. In the dim light of the lamp I saw him sitting there, an old briar pipe between his lips, his eyes fixed vacantly upon the corner of the ceiling, the blue smoke curling up from him, silent, motionless, with the light shining upon his strong-set aquiline features. So he sat as I dropped off to sleep, and so he sat when a sudden ejaculation caused me to wake up, and I found the summer sun shining into the apartment. The pipe was still between his lips, the smoke still curled upward, and the room was full of a dense tobacco haze, but nothing remained of the heap of shag which I had seen upon the previous night.

'Awake, Watson?' he asked.

'Yes.'

'Game for a morning drive?'

'Certainly.'

'Then dress. No one is stirring yet, but I know where the stable-boy sleeps, and we shall soon have the trap out.' He chuckled to himself as he spoke, his eyes twinkled, and he seemed a different man to the sombre thinker of the previous night.

As I dressed I glanced at my watch. It was no wonder that no one was stirring. It was twenty-five minutes past four. I had hardly finished when Holmes returned with the news that the boy was putting in the horse.

'I want to test a little theory of mine,' said he, pulling on his boots. 'I think, Watson, that you are now standing in the presence of one of the most absolute fools in Europe. I deserve to be kicked from here to Charing Cross. But I think I have the key of the affair now.'

'And where is it?' I asked, smiling.

'In the bathroom,' he answered. 'Oh, yes, I am not joking,' he continued, seeing my look of incredulity. 'I have just been there, and I have taken it out, and I have got it in this Gladstone bag. Come on, my boy, and we shall see whether it will not fit the lock.'

We made our way downstairs as quietly as possible, and out into the bright morning sunshine. In the road stood our horse and trap, with the half-clad stable-boy waiting at the head. We both sprang in, and away we dashed down the London Road. A few country carts were stirring, bearing in vegetables to the metropolis, but the lines of villas on either side were as silent and lifeless as some city in a dream.

'It has been in some points a singular case,' said Holmes, flicking the horse on into a gallop. 'I confess that I have been as blind as a mole, but it is better to learn wisdom late than never to learn it at all.'

In town the earliest risers were just beginning to look sleepily from their windows as we drove through the streets of the Surrey side. Passing down the Waterloo Bridge Road we crossed over the river, and dashing up Wellington Street wheeled sharply to the right and found ourselves in Bow Street. Sherlock Holmes was well known to the force, and the two constables at the door saluted him. One of them held the horse's head while the other led us in.

'Who is on duty?' asked Holmes.

'Inspector Bradstreet, sir.'

'Ah, Bradstreet, how are you?' A tall, stout official had come down the stone-flagged passage, in a peaked cap and frogged jacket.

'I wish to have a quiet word with you, Bradstreet.'

'Certainly, Mr Holmes. Step into my room here.' It was a small, office-like room, with a huge ledger upon the table, and a telephone projecting from the wall. The Inspector sat down at his desk.

'What can I do for you, Mr Holmes?'

'I called about that beggarman, Boone – the one who was charged with being concerned in the disappearance of Mr Neville St Clair, of Lee.'

'Yes. He was brought up and remanded for further inquiries.'

'So I heard. You have him here?'

'In the cells.'

'Is he quiet?'

'Oh, he gives no trouble. But he is a dirty scoundrel.'

'Dirty?'

'Yes, it is all we can do to make him wash his hands, and his face is as black as a tinker's. Well, when once his case has been settled, he will have a regular prison bath; and I think, if you saw him, you would agree with me that he needed it.'

'I should like to see him very much.'

'Would you? That is easily done. Come this way. You can leave your bag.'

'No, I think that I'll take it.'

'Very good. Come this way, if you please.' He led us down a passage, opened a barred door, passed down a winding stair, and brought us to a whitewashed corridor with a line of doors on each side.

'The third on the right is his,' said the Inspector. 'Here it is!' He quietly shot back a panel in the upper part of the door and glanced through.

'He is asleep,' said he. 'You can see him very well.'

We both put our eyes to the grating. The prisoner lay with his face towards us, in a very deep sleep, breathing slowly and heavily. He was a middle-sized man, coarsely clad as became his calling, with a coloured shirt protruding through the rent in his tattered coat. He was, as the Inspector had said, extremely dirty, but the grime which covered his face could not conceal its repulsive ugliness. A broad wheal from an old scar ran right across it from eye to chin, and by its contraction had turned up one side of the upper lip, so that three teeth were exposed in a perpetual snarl. A shock of very bright red hair grew low over his eyes and forehead.

'He's a beauty, isn't he?' said the Inspector.

'He certainly needs a wash,' remarked Holmes. 'I had an idea that he might, and I took the liberty of bringing the tools with me.' He opened the Gladstone bag as he spoke, and took out, to my astonishment, a very large bath-sponge.

'He! he! You are a funny one,' chuckled the Inspector.

'Now, if you will have the great goodness to open that door very quietly, we will soon make him cut a much more respectable figure.'

'Well, I don't know why not,' said the Inspector. 'He doesn't look a credit to the Bow Street cells, does he?' He slipped his key into the lock, and we all very quietly entered the cell. The sleeper half turned, and then settled down once more into a deep slumber. Holmes stooped to the waterjug, moistened his sponge, and then rubbed it twice vigorously across and down the prisoner's face.

'Let me introduce you', he shouted, 'to Mr Neville St Clair, of Lee, in the county of Kent.'

Never in my life have I seen such a sight. The man's face peeled off under the sponge like the bark from a tree. Gone was the coarse brown tint! Gone, too, was the horrid scar which had seamed it across, and the twisted lip which had given the repulsive sneer to the face! A twitch brought away the tangled red hair, and there, sitting up in his bed, was a pale, sad-faced, refined-looking man, black-haired and smooth-skinned, rubbing his eyes and staring about him with sleepy bewilderment. Then suddenly realising the exposure, he broke into a scream and threw himself down with his face to the pillow.

'Great heavens!' cried the Inspector, 'it is, indeed, the missing man. I know him from the photograph.'

The prisoner turned with the reckless air of a man who abandons himself to his destiny. 'Be it so,' said he. 'And pray what am I charged with?'

'With making away with Mr Neville St – Oh, come, you can't be charged with that unless they make a case of attempted suicide of it,' said the Inspector with a grin. 'Well, I have been twenty-seven years in the force, but this really takes the cake.'

'If I am Mr Neville St Clair, then it is obvious that no crime has been committed, and that, therefore, I am illegally detained.'

'No crime, but a very great error has been committed,' said Holmes. 'You would have done better to have trusted you wife.'

'It was not the wife; it was the children,' groaned the prisoner. 'God help me, I would not have them ashamed of their father. My God! What an exposure! What can I do?'

Sherlock Holmes sat down beside him on the couch and patted him kindly on the shoulder.

'If you leave it to a court of law to clear the matter up,' said he, 'of course you can hardly avoid publicity. On the other hand, if you convince the police authorities that there is no possible case against you, I do not know that there is any reason that the details should find their way into the papers. Inspector Bradstreet would, I am sure, make notes upon anything which you might tell us and submit it to the proper authorities. The case would then never go into court at all.'

'God bless you!' cried the prisoner passionately. 'I would have endured imprisonment, ay, even execution, rather than have left my miserable secret as a family blot to my children.

'You are the first who have ever heard my story. My father was a schoolmaster in Chesterfield, where I received an excellent education. I travelled in my youth, took to the stage, and finally became a reporter on an evening paper in London. One day my editor wished to have a series of articles upon begging in the metropolis, and I volunteered to supply them. There was the point from which all my adventures started. It was only by trying begging as an amateur that I could get the facts upon which to base my articles. When an actor I had, of course, learned all the secrets of making up, and had been famous in the greenroom for my skill. I took advantage now of my attainments. I painted my face, and to make myself as pitiable as possible I made a good scar and fixed one side of my lip in a twist by the aid of a small slip of flesh-coloured plaster. Then with a red head of hair, and an appropriate dress, I took my station in the business part of the city, ostensibly as a match-seller but really as a beggar. For seven hours I plied my trade, and when I returned home in the evening I found to my surprise that I had received no less than 26 shillings and 4 pence.

'I wrote my articles and thought little more of the matter until, some time later, I backed a bill for a friend and had a writ served upon me for 25 pounds. I was at my wit's end where to get the money, but a sudden idea came to me. I begged a fortnight's grace from the creditor, asked for a holiday from my employers, and spent the time in begging in the City under my disguise. In ten days I had the money and had paid the debt.

'Well, you can imagine how hard it was to settle down to arduous work at 2 pounds a week when I knew that I could earn as much in a day by smearing my face with a little paint, laying my cap on the ground, and sitting still. It was a long fight between my pride and the money, but the dollars won at last, and I threw up reporting and sat day after day in the corner which I had first chosen, inspiring pity by my ghastly face and filling my pockets with coppers. Only one man knew my secret. He was the keeper of a low den in which I used to lodge in Swandam Lane, where I could every morning emerge as a squalid beggar and in the evenings transform myself into a well-dressed man about town. This fellow, a Lascar, was well paid by me for his rooms, so that I knew that my secret was safe in his possession.

'Well, very soon I found that I was saving considerable sums of money. I do not mean that any beggar in the streets of London could earn 700 pounds a year – which is less than my average takings – but I had exceptional advantages in my power of making up, and also in a facility of repartee, which improved by practice and made me quite a recognised character in the City. All day a stream of pennies, varied by silver, poured in upon me, and it was a very bad day in which I failed to take 2 pounds.

'As I grew richer I grew more ambitious, took a house in the country, and eventually married, without anyone having a suspicion as to my real occupation. My dear wife knew that I had business in the City. She little knew what.

'Last Monday I had finished for the day and was dressing in my room above the opium den when I looked out of my window and saw, to my horror and astonishment, that my wife was standing in the street, with her eyes fixed full upon me. I gave a cry of surprise, threw up my arms to cover my face, and, rushing to my confidant, the Lascar, entreated him to prevent anyone from coming up to me. I heard her voice downstairs, but I knew that she could not ascend. Swiftly

I threw off my clothes, pulled on those of a beggar, and put on my pigments and wig. Even a wife's eyes could not pierce so complete a disguise. But then it occurred to me that there might be a search in the room, and that the clothes might betray me. I threw open the window, reopening by my violence a small cut which I had inflicted upon myself in the bedroom that morning. Then I seized my coat, which was weighted by the coppers which I had just transferred to it from the leather bag in which I carried my takings. I hurled it out of the window, and it disappeared into the Thames. The other clothes would have followed, but at that moment there was a rush of constables up the stair, and a few minutes after I found, rather, I confess, to my relief, that instead of being identified as Mr Neville St Clair, I was arrested as his murderer.

'I do not know that there is anything else for me to explain. I was determined to preserve my disguise as long as possible, and hence my preference for a dirty face. Knowing that my wife would be terribly anxious, I slipped off my ring and confided it to the Lascar at a moment when no constable was watching me, together with a hurried scrawl, telling her that she had no cause to fear.'

'That note only reached her yesterday,' said Holmes.

'Good God! What a week she must have spent!'

'The police have watched this Lascar', said Inspector Bradstreet, 'and I can quite understand that he might find it difficult to post a letter unobserved. Probably he handed it to some sailor customer of his, who forgot all about it for some days.'

'That was it,' said Holmes, nodding approvingly; 'I have no doubt of it. But have you never been prosecuted for begging?'

'Many times; but what was a fine to me?'

'It must stop here, however,' said Bradstreet. 'If the police are to hush this thing up, there must be no more of Hugh Boone.'

'I have sworn it by the most solemn oaths which a man can take.'

'In that case I think that it is probable that no further steps may be taken. But if you are found again, then all must come out. I am sure, Mr Holmes, that we are very much indebted to you for having cleared the matter up. I wish I knew how you reach your results.'

'I reached this one', said my friend, 'by sitting upon five pillows and consuming an ounce of shag. I think, Watson, that if we drive to Baker Street we shall just be in time for breakfast.'

THE END

Notes

Notes to Chapter 1

1. Martin Gray, *A Dictionary of Literary Terms* (London: Longman, 1992).
2. Roland Barthes, 'From work to text', in *Image, Music, Text*, translated by Stephen Heath (New York: Hill & Wang, 1978), p. 156.
3. Questions taken from the AQA 'English language and literature' ('The study of prose and speech') GCE A-level examination paper, June 2006.
4. Questions taken from the AQA 'English language and literature' ('Language production') GCE A-level examination paper, May 2006.

Notes to Chapter 2

1. Sir Philip Sidney, *A Defence of Poetry* (Oxford: Oxford University Press, 1978), p. 72.
2. These ideas are discussed at greater length in (for just one example) Amanda Boulter's *Writing fiction: Creative and Critical Approaches* (Palgrave, 2007).
3. The distinction between 'showing' and 'telling' is a central element of the teaching and learning of creative writing; it refers to when an author either allows the reader to make decisions and form opinions themselves (on the basis of what they are 'shown' within a text), or else when the reader is directed towards such decisions and opinions ('told') by the author, perhaps through the use of a third-person omniscient narrator.
4. Samuel Johnson, 'Selections from *The Rambler*: No. 158. Saturday, 21 September 1750', in *Samuel Johnson: Selected Poetry and Prose*, edited with an introduction and notes by Frank Brady & W. K. Wimsatt (Berkeley: University of California, 1977), p. 210.
5. Alexander Pope, 'An Essay on Criticism', in *Selected Poetry and Prose*, edited by Robin Sowerby (London: Routledge, 1992), p. 36. Subsequent references to this essay in parentheses within the main body of the text.
6. P. B Shelley, 'A Defence of Poetry', in David Lee Clark (ed.), *Shelley's Prose or the Trumpet of a Prophecy* (Albuquerque: The University of New Mexico Press, 1954), p. 296. Subsequent references to this essay in parentheses within the main body of the text.
7. Horace, 'On the Art of Poetry', in *Classical Literary Criticism*, translated with an introduction by T. S. Dorsch (Harmondsworth: Penguin, 1965), p. 89. Subsequent references to this essay in parentheses within the main body of the text.
8. Samuel Taylor Coleridge, *Biographia Literaria*, edited by Nigel Leask (London: Everyman, 1997), p. 184. Subsequent references to this publication in parentheses within the main body of the text.
9. 'HJ to C. E. Norton, March 1873' in Roger Gard (ed.), *Henry James: the Critical Heritage* (London: Routledge and Kegan Paul, 1976), p. 30.
10. Henry James, 'The Art of Fiction', in *The House of Fiction: Essays on the Novel*, edited with an introduction by Leon Edel (London: Mercury Books, 1962), p. 24.
11. Henry James, 'Criticism', in *Selected Literary Criticism*, edited by Morris Shapira (London: Heinemann, 1964), p. 135.

12. T. S. Eliot, 'To Criticize the Critic', in *To Criticize the Critic and other Writings* (London: Faber & Faber, 1978), p. 26.
13. Oscar Wilde, 'The Critic as Artist', in *The Works of Oscar Wilde*, edited by G. F. Maine (London: Collins, 1948), p. 959. Subsequent references to this essay in parentheses within the main body of the text.
14. Franco Moretti, *Atlas of the European Novel 1800–1900* (London: Verso, 1998), p. 3.
15. Thomas Carlyle, *Sartor Resartus*, edited with an introduction and notes by Kerry McSweeney and Peter Sabor (Oxford: Oxford University Press, 1987), p. 3.
16. John Fowles, *The French Lieutenant's Woman* (London: Pan, 1987), p. 85. Subsequent references to this novel in parentheses within the main body of the text.
17. Edgar Allan Poe, 'The Tell-Tale Heart', in *The Fall of the House of Usher and Other Writings*, edited with an introduction by David Galloway (Harmondsworth: Penguin, 1986), p. 277. Subsequent references to this story in parentheses within the main body of the text.
18. See Rob Pope, *Textual Intervention: Critical and Creative Strategies for Literary Studies* (London: Routledge, 1995). Subsequent references to this publication in parentheses within the main body of the text.

Notes to Chapter 3

1. Jacques Derrida, 'Ulysses' Gramophone: Hear Say Yes in Joyce', in Derek Attridge (ed.), *Acts of Literature* (New York: Routledge, 1992), pp. 253–309
2. Alexander Pope, 'An Essay on Criticism', in *Selected Poetry and Prose*, Robin Sowerby (ed.) (London: Routledge, 1992), p. 42. Subsequent references to this essay in parentheses within the main body of the text.
3. On 28th October 2005 the English Subject Centre of the UK sponsored the 'Teaching Close Reading' conference, which was intended to focus on the ways in which close reading could be relevant to modern literary criticism.
4. Aristotle, 'On the Art of Poetry', in *Classical Literary Criticism*, translated with an introduction by T. S. Dorsch (Harmondsworth: Penguin, 1965), p. 39. Subsequent references to this essay in parentheses within the main body of the text.
5. Longinus, 'On the Sublime', in *Classical Literary Criticism*, translated with an introduction by T. S. Dorsch (Harmondsworth: Penguin, 1965), p. 108.
6. Samuel Taylor Coleridge, *Biographia Literaria* [1817], edited by Nigel Leask (London: Everyman, 1997), p. 186.
7. I. A. Richards, *Practical Criticism: a Study of Literary Judgement* (1929) (London: Routledge, 1964), p. 13. Subsequent references to this publication in parentheses within the main body of the text.
8. I. A. Richards, *How to Read a Page: a Course in Effective Reading with an Introduction to a Hundred Great Words* (London: Routledge & Kegan Paul, 1954), p. 11. Subsequent references to this publication in parentheses within the main body of the text.
9. See (for example) Wimsatt's *The Verbal Icon: Studies in the Meaning of Poetry* (Lexington: University of Kentucky Press, 1954).
10. John Crowe Ransom, *The New Criticism* (Westport, CT: Greenwood Press, 1979), p. xi. Subsequent references to this publication in parentheses within the main body of the text.
11. See Ransom, *The New Criticism*, p. 90–2 for a more detailed discussion of these contexts.
12. Cleanth Brooks, *The Well Wrought Urn: Studies in the Structure of Poetry* (London:

Methuen, 1968), p. vi. Subsequent references to this publication in parentheses within the main body of the text.

13. F. R. Leavis, *The Great Tradition: George Eliot. Henry James. Joseph Conrad* (London: Chatto & Windus, 1962), p. 5. Subsequent references to this publication in parentheses within the main body of the text.

14. Jacques Derrida, *Of Grammatology*, translated by Gayatri Chakravorty Spivak (Johns Hopkins University Press, 1976), p. 158.

15. T. S. Eliot, 'The Frontiers of Criticism', in *On Poetry and Poets* (London: Faber & Faber, 1965), p. 113. Subsequent references to this essay in parentheses within the main body of the text.

Notes to Chapter 4

1. Samuel Johnson, 'Selections from *The Rambler*: No. 60. Saturday, 13 October 1750', in *Samuel Johnson: Selected Poetry and Prose*, edited with an introduction and notes by Frank Brady & W. K. Wimsatt (Berkeley: University of California, 1977), p. 182.

2. Samuel Johnson, 'Thomas Gray', in *Lives of the English Poets: Volume 2 Congreve to Gray* (London: J. M. Dent, 1961), p. 388.

3. Samuel Johnson, 'Abraham Cowley', in *Lives of the English Poets: Volume 1 Cowley to Prior* (London: J. M. Dent, 1961), p. 1.

4. T. S. Eliot, 'The Frontiers of Criticism', in *On Poetry and Poets* (London: Faber & Faber, 1965), p. 112. Subsequent references to this essay in parentheses within the main body of the text.

5. Roland Barthes, 'The Death of the Author', in *Modern Literary Theory: a Reader*, 2nd edition, Philip Rice & Patricia Waugh (eds) (London: Edward Arnold, 1992), p. 118. The essay was originally published in Barthes' own *Image, Music, Text*. Subsequent references to this essay in parentheses within the main body of the text.

6. Tony Bennett, 'Texts, Readers, Reading Formations', in Philip Rice & Patricia Waugh (eds), *Modern Literary Theory: a Reader*, 2nd edition (London: Edward Arnold, 1992), p. 211. Subsequent references to this essay in parentheses within the main body of the text.

7. Stanley Fish, *Is there a Text in this Class?* (Cambridge, MA: Harvard University Press, 1980), p. 164.

8. Roland Barthes, *S/Z*, translated by Richard Miller (New York: Hill & Wang, 1974), p. 4. Subsequent references to this publication in parentheses within the main body of the text.

9. Stella Tillyard, *Aristocrats: Caroline, Emily, Louisa and Sarah Lennox 1740–1832* (London: Farrar Straus and Giroux, 1994), p. xi.

10. For an expanded reading see Kathleen Constable, *A Stranger Within the Gates* (2000).

Notes to Chapter 5

1. P. B Shelley, 'Preface to *Prometheus Unbound*', in David Lee Clark (ed.), *Shelley's Prose or the Trumpet of a Prophecy* (Albuquerque: The University of New Mexico Press, 1954), p. 327.

2. T. S. Eliot, 'Tradition and the Individual Talent', in *Points of View* (London: Faber & Faber, 1944), p. 25. Subsequent references to this essay in parentheses within the main body of the text.

3. Plato, *The Republic*, translated with an introduction by Desmond Lee (Harmondsworth: Penguin, 1987), p. 133. Subsequent references in parentheses within the main body of the text.

4. P. B Shelley, 'A Defence of Poetry', in David Lee Clark (ed.), *Shelley's Prose or the Trumpet of a Prophecy* (Albuquerque: The University of New Mexico Press, 1954), p. 297. Subsequent references to this essay in parentheses within the main body of the text.

5. Arnold, *Culture and Anarchy*, in *Matthew Arnold: Selected Prose*, edited with an introduction by P. J. Keating (Harmondsworth: Penguin, 1987), p. 221. Subsequent references in parentheses within the main body of the text.

6. T. S. Eliot, 'The Frontiers of Criticism', in *On Poetry and Poets* (London: Faber & Faber, 1965), p. 117

7. Toni Morrison, *Beloved* (London: Picador, 1988), p. 3. Subsequent references in parentheses within the main body of the text.

Notes to Chapter 6

1. T. S. Eliot, 'The Frontiers of Criticism', in *On Poetry and Poets* (London: Faber & Faber, 1965), p. 104.

2. Plato, *The Republic*, translated with an introduction by Desmond Lee (Harmondsworth: Penguin, 1987), p. 149. Subsequent references in parentheses within the main body of the text.

3. Aristotle, 'On the Art of Poetry', in *Classical Literary Criticism*, translated with an introduction by T. S. Dorsch (Harmondsworth: Penguin, 1965), p. 69. Subsequent references in parentheses within the main body of the text.

4. Horace, 'On the Art of Poetry', in *Classical Literary Criticism*, translated with an introduction by T. S. Dorsch (Harmondsworth: Penguin, 1965), p. 80. Subsequent references in parentheses within the main body of the text.

5. Longinus, 'On the Sublime', in *Classical Literary Criticism*, translated with an introduction by T. S. Dorsch (Harmondsworth: Penguin, 1965), p. 100. Subsequent references in parentheses within the main body of the text.

6. Sir Philip Sidney, *A Defence of Poetry* (Oxford: Oxford University Press, 1978), p. 25. Subsequent references in parentheses within the main body of the text.

7. Samuel Johnson, 'George Stepney', in *Lives of the English Poets: Volume 1 Cowley to Prior* (London: J. M. Dent, 1961), p. 272.

8. Samuel Johnson, 'Abraham Cowley', in *Lives of the English Poets: Volume 2 Congreve to Gray* (London: J. M. Dent, 1961), p. 298.

9. Wordsworth, 'Advertisement, composed July 1798', in Duncan Wu (ed.), *Romanticism: an Anthology* (Oxford: Blackwell, 1994), p. 166. Subsequent references in parentheses within the main body of the text.

10. Wordsworth, 'Preface to *Lyrical Ballads*', in Duncan Wu (ed.), *Romanticism: An Anthology* (Oxford: Blackwell, 1994), p. 250. Subsequent references in parentheses within the main body of the text.

11. Samuel Taylor Coleridge, *Biographia Literaria* [1817], edited by Nigel Leask (London: Everyman, 1997), p. 184. Subsequent references to this publication in parentheses within the main body of the text.

12. P. B Shelley, 'A Defence of Poetry', in David Lee Clark (ed.), *Shelley's Prose or the Trumpet of a Prophecy* (Albuquerque: The University of New Mexico Press, 1954), p. 295. Subsequent references to this essay in parentheses within the main body of the text.

13. P. B Shelley, 'Preface to *Laon and Cythna; or, the Revolution of the Golden City: a Vision*

of the Nineteenth Century', in David Lee Clark (ed.), *Shelley's Prose or the Trumpet of a Prophecy* (Albuquerque: The University of New Mexico Press, 1954), p. 316.

14. T. S. Eliot, 'Tradition and the Individual Talent', in *Points of View* (London: Faber & Faber, 1944), p. 24. Subsequent references to this essay in parentheses within the main body of the text.

15. The essay was originally published in Marianne Hirsch and Evelyn Fox Keller (eds), *Conflicts in Feminism* (New York: Routledge, 1990).

16. Sigmund Freud, 'Civilization and its Discontents', *The Freud Reader*, edited by Peter Gay (London: Vintage, 1995), p. 771. Subsequent references to this essay in parentheses within the main body of the text.

17. Teresa de Lauretis, 'Upping the Anti [sic] in Feminist Theory', in Simon During (ed.), *The Cultural Studies Reader* (London: Routledge, 1994), p. 75

Bibliography

Arnold, M., *Matthew Arnold: Selected Prose*, edited with an introduction by P. J. Keating
(Harmondsworth: Penguin, 1987).

Attridge, D. (ed.), *Acts of Literature* (New York: Routledge, 1992).

Barthes, R., *S/Z*, translated by Richard Miller (New York: Hill & Wang, 1974).

—— *Image, Music, Text*, translated by Stephen Heath (New York: Hill & Wang, 1978).

Boulter, A., *Writing Fiction: Creative and Critical Approaches* (Basingstoke: Palgrave, 2007).

Brooks, C., *The Well-Wrought Urn: Studies in the Structure of Poetry* (London: Methuen,
1968).

Carlyle, T., *Sartor Resartus*, edited with an introduction and notes by Kerry Sweeney and Peter
Sabor (Oxford: Oxford University Press, 1987).

Clark, D. L. (ed.), *Shelley's Prose or the Trumpet of a Prophecy* (Albuquerque: The University of
New Mexico Press, 1954).

—— *Classical Literary Criticism*, translated with an introduction by T. S. Dorsch
(Harmondsworth: Penguin, 1965).

Coleridge, S. T., *Biographia Literaria*, Nigel Leask (ed.) (London: Everyman, 1997).

Derrida, J., *Of Grammatology*, translated by Gayatri Chakravorty Spivak (Baltimore: Johns
Hopkins University Press, 1976).

During, S. (ed.), *The Cultural Studies Reader* (London: Routledge, 1994).

Eliot, T. S., *Points of View* (London: Faber & Faber, 1944).

—— *On Poetry and Poets* (London: Faber & Faber, 1965).

—— *To Criticize the Critic and Other Writings* (London: Faber & Faber, 1978).

Fish, S., *Is there a Text in this Class?* (Cambridge, MA: Harvard University Press, 1980).

Fowles, J., *The French Lieutenant's Woman* (London: Pan, 1987).

Freud, S., 'Civilization and its Discontents', *The Freud Reader*, edited by Peter Gay (London:
Vintage, 1995).

Gard, R. (ed.), *Henry James: the Critical Heritage* (London: Routledge and Kegan Paul, 1976).

Gray, M., *A Dictionary of Literary Terms* (Harlow: Longman York, 1992).

Hirsch, M., and Evelyn Fox Keller (eds), *Conflicts in Feminism* (New York: Routledge, 1990).

James, H., *The House of Fiction: Essays on the Novel*, edited with an introduction by Leon Edel
(London: Mercury Books, 1962).

—— *Selected Literary Criticism*, edited by Morris Shapira (London: Heinemann, 1964).

Johnson, S., *Lives of the English Poets: Volume 1 Cowley to Prior* (London: J. M. Dent, 1961).

—— *Lives of the English Poets: Volume 2 Congreve to Gray* (London: J. M. Dent, 1961).

—— *Samuel Johnson: Selected Poetry and Prose*, edited, with an introduction and notes by
Frank Brady & W. K. Wimsatt (Berkeley: University of California, 1977).

Leavis, F. R., *The Great Tradition: George Eliot. Henry James. Joseph Conrad* (London: Chatto
& Windus, 1962).

Moretti, F., *Atlas of the European Novel 1800–1900* (London: Verso, 1998).

Morrison, T., *Beloved* (London: Picador, 1988).

Plato, *The Republic*, translated with an introduction by Desmond Lee (Harmondsworth: Penguin, 1987).

Poe, E. A., *The Fall of the House of Usher and Other Writings*, edited with an introduction by David Galloway (Harmondsworth: Penguin, 1986).

Pope, A., *Selected Poetry and Prose*, edited by Robin Sowerby (London: Routledge, 1992).

Pope, R., *Textual Intervention: Critical and Creative Strategies for Literary Studies* (London: Routledge, 1995).

Ransom, J. C., *The New Criticism* (Westport, CT: Greenwood Press, 1979).

Rice, P. and Patricia Waugh (eds) *Modern Literary Theory: a Reader*, 2nd edn (London: Edward Arnold, 1992).

Richards, I. A., *Practical Criticism: a Study of Literary Judgement* (London: Routledge, 1964).

—— *How to Read a Page: a Course in Effective Reading with an Introduction to a Hundred Great Words* (London: Routledge & Kegan Paul, 1954).

Scholes, R., *Textual Power: Theory and the Teaching of English* (New Haven, CT: Yale University Press, 1985).

Sidney, Sir P., *A Defence of Poetry* (Oxford: Oxford University Press, 1978).

Tillyard, S., *Aristocrats: Caroline, Emily, Louisa and Sarah Lennox 1740–1832* (London: Farrar Straus and Giroux, 1994).

Wilde, O., *The Works of Oscar Wilde*, edited by G. F. Maine (London: Collins, 1948).

Wimsatt, W. K., *The Verbal Icon: Studies in the Meaning of Poetry* (Lexington: University of Kentucky Press, 1954).

Wu, D. (ed.), *Romanticism: an Anthology* (Oxford: Blackwell, 1994).

Index